FOREWARD

Over the last 50 years of broadcasting early in the morning, then napping in the afternoon, during the evening and on weekends I have had the opportunity to speak at various functions, large and small, from Inuvik to Las Vegas, and in Alberta from Fort McMurray to Taber. As I have come down from the stage, on many occasions, people have said to me, "Bob – you have got to write a book!"

So, I did. Five, in fact. My best known is Audreys' best-seller *Welcome to Radio*, the story of my life in broadcasting.

My dad taught me, as outlined in that book, that you can learn to do anything you put your mind to. He also made it plain as he moved from job to job in my younger years that you should never depend on one employer. They can go broke or get bought out, or anything can happen that will cost you your job, and your main responsibility is to feed your family, so you better have something else going on the side.

My dad did a lot of that, and sometimes I would go along to help. In his day it was called "moonlighting." Today, those extra jobs are called "side hustles."

In my broadcasting career, I saw many lose their jobs as the economy shifted and stations were bought and sold, but I somehow survived; sometimes with a change in compensation, offset by playing in a band.

Thanks, Dad.

This book tells of many different speaking engagements, bizarre things that happened in the background as wedding DJ, how and why I became a certified auctioneer and a professional ventriloquist and relaxed by playing bluegrass music.

As 630 CHED'S morning host Shaye Ganam once said, on-air, "Bob has a lot of side hustles."

I will also show you a different side of some people you have heard of who were also out of the office, speaking and so on.

I am also pleased to share some heart-felt thoughts from former 630 CHED morning host, Bruce Bowie, on his life in broadcasting.

There is an important life-lesson I learned at a funeral.

While you're stuck at home by the pandemic, I'll take you on some past cruises and share some interesting and somewhat bizarre extended road trips.

As in any project, there are people to thank, like Rob Hislop who designed this book's cover and did much of the excellent photography you are about to see; my nephew Steven Layton, a Lethbridge photographer who sharpened up some of the photos supplied by people whose stories I'll share; and my daughter Debi Watson who proof-read the early manuscript.

Many edits were done by my son, Chris, a Language Arts/Music/Band/Drama/Guitar/Drums/Bass/Math/17 other things teacher. Need to know the proper use of a comma? See his "Comma Song Mr. Layton" on YouTube.

The final edits were done by Wilhelmina McKeddie, whose sharp eyes would be a benefit to any aspiring writer.

And, most of all, my thanks to my wife Marg for her patience as I spent countless hours researching and remembering and rewriting and learning how to work with Amazon.

We are anxious for the pandemic to end so we can share the stories for this book at your gathering.

One more thing you need to understand before you read this book:

I write like I talk. Now, for an essay, I might have to write, 'I write the same way in which I speak,' but this is not a book of essays; it is a book of stories of my side-hustles and what I learned along the way. My listeners know my voice, and one of the things they often say is how they can hear my voice when reading my books.

Enjoy!

"I'll puke in your pocket!"

Chapter 1 - The accidental DJ..................................1

Chapter 2 - You get what you pay for....................8

Chapter 3 – Hotels..53

Chapter 4 - Public Speaking..................................56

Chapter 5 - Watchagonnabidfor'em?....................72

Chapter 6 - Who said it best?................................78

Chapter 7 – Travelling...102

Chapter 8 - Taxi lessons......................................126

Chapter 9 - Hang loose!......................................133

Chapter 10 - The eyes have it.............................137

Chapter 11 – Keep your mouth shut...................148

Chapter 12 - Court stories...................................158

Chapter 13 – Conventions...................................170

Chapter 14 - I Love cars.....................................176

Chapter 15 – Christmas.......................................184

Chapter 16 - On stage..195

Chapter 17 – Hospitals..204

Chapter 18 – Snow angels..208

Chapter 19 – Lessons to learn.....................................212

Chapter 20 - A true radio legend................................221

Chapter 21 - Grandpa's gift...229

Chapter 22 - Ducks on the lake...................................233

Chapter 23 – Intercourse...240

Chapter 24 – Time or money......................................246

Chapter 25 – Rwanda Rob...256

Chapter 26 - Pandemic poetry....................................266

Chapter 27 – Awards..283

Chapter 28 – And one final thought..........................301

The accidental DJ

Chapter 1

It was noon on Valentine's Day in the early 1980s. I arrived home for lunch after working since the wee hours of the morning to find my daughter Debi quite upset. She went to St. Francis Xavier High School and there was supposed to be a dance right after school. They had the gym beautifully decorated, and activities planned, but the social convener had forgotten to hire a Disc Jockey. They had called every DJ company in town and they were all booked solid – not a DJ to be had anywhere.

"Is there anything we can do, Dad?" she pleaded.

I wondered what she might be thinking. We did have a family band, The Layton Aggregation. Debi was on rhythm guitar and vocals, my son, David, on drums, Marg on keyboards, I played bass, and later, Roy Narten would join us on lead guitar and vocals. I knew she was not thinking of us playing, because our music was more for weddings with country and waltzes and polkas and some rock.

But we did have lots of equipment, speakers, amps, PA system, and so on. What we were lacking was a mixer to go seamlessly from one song to another, and we did not have the music of the day her class would want.

Always up for a challenge, I thought about it for a few minutes and told her there *was* a possible way we could do that dance, but it would not be very pretty. In fact, it might get ugly.

It was not like we had not faced music challenges before. There was the dance at a rural hall where we discovered the bag containing the drumsticks had been left behind. I checked with the local school to see if they had a music room with some drumsticks, but they did not. I looked outside at the trees to see if there was a thin, brittle branch – that's how desperate we were. The family was on the edge of tears when I saw the answer across the hall in the kitchen.

Some cooks were using long-handled wooden spoons for mixing. I went and borrowed a couple. David was skeptical because they would not bounce right, and besides, it would look stupid.

My dad, once a carnival man, had given me some insight into how they sold illusions like *the headless lady* to the public. I decided to give it a go. I went out on stage and asked how many people had seen the music video where a drummer was getting a unique sound by using wooden spoons instead of regular drumsticks. Surprisingly, a fellow put up his hand. I explained that David was going to do the same thing and away we went.

Attention DJs: it's OK if you grimace as you hear how this St. FX dance was put together on the fly, and I mean *on the fly*.

I told Debi to spread the word among her friends to bring their favorite dance cassette, since that was what pop music was being played on in those days. CDs would come later. I put our

PA system on the stage and plugged a microphone into the amp along with a single cassette player, which was all we had at home.

As the cassettes arrived on stage, I would find the right song and stop it on the first note. Then, using my index finger, I would roll the tape back a quarter turn so it would not sound slow starting up. Some of the students helped by cuing up their own songs before handing them up to me.

Wondering how bad this would turn out to be, I grabbed the mic and wished everyone at St. FX a happy Valentine's Day and started the first song. Had there been a proper mixer, I would have caught the fade of the first song and begun the second one, but that would not be possible, and I had to become a multi-tasker. As the first song began to fade, I talked about how great the decorations were and called for some applause while I quickly changed cassettes, dropping the first one on the table and starting the second one.

In my mind, I had a list of comments I could make to cover the lack of equipment. Some of the students wanted their favorite song played more than once and I was happy to do whatever would make them happy.

I think I was sweating a bit as we got down to the final song of what I was sure was the most unprofessional and clunky DJ this group had ever seen. My plan was to have Debi and my son, Dave, help me get the equipment out to the car and get out of there as quickly as we could before anyone remarked on my poor abilities as a DJ. I hoped they would realize this was an emergency and not be too hard on Debi.

As the dance ended, I quickly started ripping out sound and electrical cords and motioned to Dave to hurry it up because we needed to get out of there.

There was a problem. A teacher wanted to speak with me, as did a couple of students, and they were up on the stage, in the way of our escape. The teacher wanted to thank us for all the work we did putting this together at the last minute. She said the students would also like to say something, and they took me totally by surprise.

They said this was the best dance ever, and I was the best DJ because I did what others would not. First, every song I played was a request. Other DJs brought their own playlist and it seemed they seldom played requests. Second, I played the most popular songs more than once – other DJs had told them that was not the right way to do a dance. They enjoyed my comments between songs, especially in congratulating the committees that put this dance together. And the biggest surprise of all – they liked the quick pause between every song, because it gave them a chance to change partners if they wanted. It was awkward to try to change partners sometimes when the songs were so tightly mixed.

What a DJ lesson that was!

They hoped we would be available for their dance at the end of the term. Unfortunately, with all our other commitments, we were not. While I appreciated their surprise comments, I did not really want to go through that again. Still, it would not be the last time I would be called to St. FX in what seemed like an emergency.

I was at work, busy on a story when I got a call from the principal's office. I was told that Debi was having a problem and that I needed to come right away.

"You mean I need to leave work? Is it that serious?"

"Yes."

They would not give me any more information over the phone, saying it was best they talk with me in person, and that, no, in response to my question, an ambulance was not required.

As I drove to the school, I wondered what could be wrong. I recalled how she got into that school. She did not want to go to Jasper Place Composite High School. I had been to JP many times and it was quite a hive of activity. Even when classes were on, there were students hanging out in the hallway and goofing off. I wondered how that could be allowed.

Debi especially wanted to attend the drama classes at St. FX. She had heard they were excellent. The problem was, it is a Catholic School, and we are not Catholic. She had friends who were not Catholic, and they were allowed in, so I went over to the office to find out how to get her enrolled.

The office staff assured me she would be welcome, but they were not allowed, for some reason, to tell me how to get her in.

I was shaking my head as I left. Just as I was about to open the door to leave, a teacher came up quietly beside me and said, "If you want your daughter to go here, go down to city hall and change your school taxes from 'Public' to 'Public and Separate.'" Then she was gone.

I did. Debi was admitted.

Now, here I was again parking in front of St. Francis Xavier. I bounded up the steps, opened the door and quickly walked in. The first thing I noticed was that the hallways were empty. No students hanging around, acting stupid, or staring at strangers as I had seen in other places.

As I passed the first classroom, a teacher noticed me and came right out, walking with me. She asked if she could help me.

"It's OK," I said, 'I'm just going to the office."

She replied, in stride with me, "I'll walk with you."

I entered the office to find out what the problem with Debi was. The person in charge looked me straight in the eye and said, "She did not finish her homework last night."   I could see he was not kidding.

I was dumbfounded. It's not like me to be left searching for words, but I wanted to say exactly the right thing about being called away from work to hear something like this.

Accurately reading the look on my face, he wisely jumped right in with, "We think your daughter's education is important, don't you?"

I could only agree with him and thought the best way to leave the office gracefully would be to promise him this would never happen again.

He smiled just a tiny little bit and said, "It never does."

And it never happened again.

At least, as far as I know.

You get what you pay for...
Chapter 2

Somehow, the word got around and after a few calls about playing dances, I started doing some for the teens at our church. I had purchased a mixer and some lighting and a couple of speakers that looked great on stage. They looked powerful.

Turned out they were not that great. I knew nothing about buying this type of speaker, I had just bought what looked good and did not cost too much. It was at a teen dance in Sherwood Park where they asked me to crank up the volume, which I did – and blew out one of the speakers. I moved the other one to the middle of the stage and finished the dance that way. I was surprised; no one seemed to care but me.

I had a couple more dances on the calendar, and I could not let this happen again. I went to a music store, Long and McQuade, and looked at the best they had. Each cabinet had two large speakers and a horn. The label said 1,000 watts! No way these would blow out on stage, but they sure could blow out my wallet. This was way beyond any expense I could imagine. What to do? What to do?

There were less expensive speakers in the store, but they looked like nothing compared to these, and I did not want to be embarrassed by another failure in front of a crowd.

I held my breath and said I would take them and that huge amp that would drive them. The manager came over and congratulated me on buying the best, but it did not take the sting out of the price tag. I started feeling buyer's remorse on the way home. I wondered if maybe I should just have gotten out of the business instead of going into debt like this. What was I thinking?

That Saturday night I set up for a wedding dance at the Petroleum Club. I made sure I got there early so I could test those speakers out in a big hall. They sounded fantastic. I went out front to have a look at them and they were the best thing I had seen on any stage by any DJ. I was deep in thought when a man came up and asked if I was the DJ. I nodded.

Asking if I had a card, he said, "I'd like to book you for my wedding in three months."

"But you haven't even seen my show..." I started.

"Don't have to. I'm looking at your equipment and I can see how serious you are about what you do. Is that date open?"

You bet it was, and many more after that paid the equipment off quicker than I ever thought possible, but I had some other tough lessons to learn along the way. Contrary to the saying, I would discover that the customer was not always right.

One of my first weddings was at a local golf club. We had been booked by the mother of the bride, who gave us the three opening numbers. We did not meet the bride and groom, which

I thought was odd. Mom asked if we had lots of waltzes. I explained we had enough music of every kind that covered rock, country, polka, and, yes, we had lots of waltzes. She nodded, signed the contract and the meeting was over.

The reception seemed standard with the usual speeches and toasts. We were surveying the guests and noticed lots in their early 20s, so we were lining up the right music. When our turn came, we announced the first dance: "For the happiest couple in the world today!" Then came the next dance where the wedding party joined in, and then the dance with the bride and her dad and the groom and his mom. The next dance I said was "only for family and friends." Some people looked like they were processing that for a bit, and then the floor filled up to a medium tempo tune.

After that, I introduced Dave, and I made the promise that we were playing totally by request. "Foxtrot, polka, two-step, rock, Latin – you name it, we'll play it." We had been receiving requests during the supper and had those songs lined up. I announced, "And our first request of the night – the Stones – Satisfaction!" As that all-familiar opening riff filled the room, the floor was packed.

The bride's mother strode up behind the DJ table and said with a frown on her face, "What do you think you are doing?"

"Uh – starting the… uh… dance… is something wrong?"

"Yes – something is wrong! I asked if you had lots of waltzes and you said you did! What is this terrible music you're playing?"

I was caught totally off-guard. "Well, we played three waltzes off the top, and now we are playing by request. We'll play a little of each kind of music and then there will be more waltzes later. Is that okay?" I asked.

"No, it's not. I want waltzes *now*."

"But that would be a lot of waltzes, and that's not really what the guests want... and..."

"I don't care what my daughter's stupid friends want. I'm paying you, and I want waltzes, right now."

A novice DJ, I was not sure how to handle this one. I needed some musical clarification. "So, how many... waltzes... do you...?"

'I want all waltzes. *All* waltzes. Do you understand?"

No, I did not understand, but I was brought up hearing an old saying, "He who pays the piper calls the tune."

I went to waltzes. All waltzes. I don't know if the Emeralds ever got so much play unless they were doing the dance themselves.

The guests turned on us, demanding to know where their requests were. I tried to explain what was going on but those who came to the table were having none of it. One asked for our business card so they could make sure they never made the mistake of hiring us. Others told us we were the worst wedding DJs they had ever seen, and people started hugging the bride and groom and making excuses about having to leave early, and then the hall was emptying out. It wasn't even ten o'clock yet.

Soon, the dance floor was empty. A few seniors danced a waltz or two and then sat down. The mother came over and told us to pack up and go home. I started to apologize for losing the crowd, but she told me she had no intention of sitting there all night and she was glad it was over.

I have always wondered how that marriage turned out. My mother-in-law was a wonderful woman, and I never understood comedians who were so hard on mothers-in-law and their supposed meddling.

Now, I understood how commandeering some might be.

I also understood that if we were going to provide entertainment I was proud of, while giving the happy couple and their friends a dance they would talk about the next day, I was going to have to be more assertive with future clients.

Despite the first unhappy guests, bookings kept coming in and I found myself protecting my reputation. One bride was adamant that there be no country music played at her wedding. It was going to be more of a "high class" wedding at a major hotel. (This is where I hear Garth Brooks in the back of my mind singing, "Blame it all on my roots, I showed up in boots, and ruined your black-tie affair…")

I explained to her that I put request cards on every table, and the number one requested music I get in Edmonton is country music. She was having none of it and said she would find a different DJ, even though she had told me at the beginning she wanted Layton Music because several of her friends had seen us at other functions and said we had the best music mix and knew how to keep the floor full.

A few days later she called back and asked very hesitantly if I could, maybe, somehow... keep the country music to... say... a minimum. I asked if she had tried other DJs. She had, but they were also not interested in a wedding dance with no country music. I told her the only promise I could make was to only play country music that was requested. Perhaps, I suggested, her guests would not want any. She agreed they most likely would not. She thought she knew them that well.

When the wedding dance came, the requests were pretty much what I had expected. A little of every music genre and lots of country. We had to smile as we saw people drag the bride onto the floor to learn to do a line dance. Bless her heart, she kept on smiling.

As I sat in the living room of another bride and groom to be, the lady said there was something she hated at every dance that the DJ foisted upon people and seemed to be making them do, and it was not going to happen at her wedding. "Do not play that stupid Bird Dance!" I explained to her that we only play by request, and that there will be several wanting the Bird Dance. We not only had the great version by the Emeralds, but we also had an extended international version. She reluctantly agreed and suggested maybe I could play it while she was out for a smoke or something.

That night as we were setting up, a bridal messenger arrived to tell us there was to be *no Bird Dance*. The look on my face was enough for the messenger to add, "She knew you would not be happy, but she's hiring you and you have to obey her instructions."

Usually, as you get closer to the end of the dance, people ask what happened to their request. You can only play about 40-45 songs in a night, and you may have 60 requests, so that's when you are at your most apologetic. I did not want to apologize for something I could have controlled.

In the first hour of the dance, a sweet little girl came up and asked for the Bird Dance, saying she wanted to do it, and her family's whole table had sent her up to make the request. She pointed at them and they waved.

A little devil on my shoulder whispered in my ear. I bent down and told her that the bride approves all the music, and she would have to go ask her if it was okay if we played it.

She happily skipped across the dance floor to where the bride was talking with some people and tugged on her dress. I watched carefully as she spoke to the bride and watched the look on the bride's face turn to one of helpless resignation. She thought for just a second, then looked across the floor at me and reluctantly mouthed the words, "Play it." To our great surprise, as a huge circle formed, she joined in.

Being a DJ is not all fun and dancing. It is highly competitive. At some dances, someone will arrive to say they are also a DJ and are related to the bride or groom and have no idea why they did not get the job. I would ask them to observe the dancers and tell me what type of music I should play next. Do they want to polka, or are they ready for a waltz? The answer was often, "I don't know, I just play what I feel like playing."

That would explain it.

We had played a couple of gigs at a rural hall to much applause. Weeks later, I was stopped in a mall by two young men. They were so excited! They recognized me from a previous dance. Their parents had helped them buy DJ equipment and also helped them get the next dance at the same hall.

I asked if they had the right music. They thought so. I suggested that for a wedding dance at that particular hall, they needed a good supply of two-steps, some Emeralds' polkas, some old-time waltzes, and some 80s dance music, for starters. I was about to add more, but I was cut short as one of the boys waved me off. "I don't play any of that old crap – I'm playing rap!" His friend, smiling wide, nodded in agreement and away they went.

It was quite a while after that meeting that I ran into the smiley one. I asked him how the dance went, and he wasn't smiling any more. He told me how no one was dancing to the best rap available. Dancers were demanding other types of music. One big guy, who may have had too much to drink, wanted a two-step. When told they didn't have any, he pushed them aside and had a look at their tray of CDs. After going through it, the boy told me, he picked it up and started heading for the door. They followed, protesting, but he went out the door and dumped the CDs into a snowdrift.

Then he backed his big pick-up right to the door and put a CD on and cranked the volume, and as the boys tried to recover their music from the snow, people were dancing and laughing.

There were several times when people who I think must have wanted the gig we got tried to sabotage us. They would send up a list of a half a dozen songs we knew would clear the floor and leave us looking inept. They were songs that just did not, as one album cover says, "Shoot musical bullets at the dancer's feet." Later, the person would come up and demand those songs be played. When I showed no interest, they might tell me something like, "You don't know this crowd – these are the songs they are waiting for – let's get them on! I will be right here waiting to hear you play them."

I was sure these songs were wrong for this crowd, but what if he was right? I got my answer as I watched him go back to his table, put on his coat, and leave. I thought he might be going for a smoke, but he never came back.

A few dances later, it happened again with songs I knew were wrong. The fellow was very insistent, maybe too much so. As he was leaving the stage, the song was fading out and I took the mic. "Ladies and gentlemen, are you having a good time?"

Huge applause.

"Are we too loud?"

Big No-o-o-o.

"Are you getting the music you want?"

More applause.

"I'd like you to meet a gentleman who was just on stage – he's standing right there. Wave to him. I want to thank him for giving me a list of songs he says you all want to dance to…"

More applause.

I named the songs.

There was silence.

I said, "Maybe later," and went into a guaranteed floor filler.

The guy left. At the end of the night, the bride and groom asked if I knew the fellow with the strange list. I did not. They did not know him either.

Remember to RSVP

We were playing a wedding at the Royal Glenora Club, which is a beautiful place to have a wedding. Cocktail hour was over, and the guests were invited to come into the dining room and sit down. There were place cards at each plate, and people walked around and found theirs.

Some people walked around the room a couple of times and not finding their names, they just stood against the wall, looking very perplexed. Eventually, the father of the bride took the mic and said, "If there's no place setting with your name on it, it's because you did not bother to RSVP. So, you will not be eating."

You should have seen the glances of blame the husbands and wives were shooting at each other. Then the man with the mic said, "Just kidding, the long tables on the side with no names are for you."

But that was not the only thing he did. At one point he stood up and said, "I'd now like to read you the annual report of my company." And he did. And it was lengthy. He went on about stocks and bonds and earnings before taxes and interest and something else no one understood, and it went on and on and on. People's eyes were glazing over. The bride and groom just looked straight ahead, showing no concern.

Finally, he was done, and he said, "I know you're thinking that was pretty boring, but my accountant tells me that because I read the annual report here, I can write this whole evening off my income tax."

I did not know if that was true or just a joke, so I went to our accounting department with the question. They were not sure, but if you own a company and this works, you're welcome.

My kids were hoping we could DJ more dances at schools. I called some schools to offer our services of what was then the Thunder and Lightning Music Show. To highlight the name, I had the guys at 630 CHED make me a splitter to play between songs that was the sound of thunder and lightning. It was in stereo, of course, and would thunder back and forth from speaker to speaker.

The schools all said they had already hired DJs to cover the year's dances, so we were out of luck. At the radio station they were doing a lot of surveys, asking what the audience did and did not like about 630 CHED's sound. I decided to do the same for the music show.

I sent a survey to every school, asking what they liked and did not like about their DJs. The response was very enlightening, and reminiscent of what I had been told at St. FX.

I sent a follow-up to the survey, based on their responses, explaining that we were not like other school DJs. We played by request and did not have a set playlist. We welcomed students on stage, especially during the Village People's "YMCA." They could line up across the front and show us what they had.

And we added something else. We invited them in the week before the dance to choose a guest DJ, someone they thought would be great, and we would let them introduce some of the songs.

We started getting bookings.

What's new?

We had to upgrade this side hustle with better lights and sound equipment. After hauling around cases of cassettes, something new was on the market – CDs. They were great because you didn't have to cue them, and the sound was supposed to be so much better, but it meant investing in your music all over again.

It was at Jasper Place High School that I tried an experiment. I had "Jump" by the Pointer Sisters on both cassette and CD. I loaded the cassette on one side and the CD on the other. I explained to the students that I would start both players at once, and then switch back and forth, motioning to the left and right as I did so, allowing them to hear the difference in sound quality.

When the song was over, I asked for a show of hands, did the left side sound best, or did the right sound better? Which was it?

Bottom line: They could not hear any difference.

What's old is new again

The year the movie *Ferris Bueller's Day Off* came out, I was at a junior high school dance, when a teacher (or maybe it was the principal), wearing industrial earmuffs, came on stage with a young girl. He said she had a request. She asked me, since the movie had just come out, if I had "Twist and Shout" by the Beatles, *yet*. I told her "No," then paused as she looked disappointed, and added: "I have it *still*." She didn't get it, but the principal did. I played it next.

Then came a call from a junior high that wanted a dance but could not afford it. I suggested if they could arrange for a crew of strong boys to haul in my speakers and lighting, I could give them a break on the price. An agreement was made, and I arrived that day and went to the principal's office. I explained to the person at the front desk what the deal was. She said the boys were in gym class and she'd have the teacher send me the right ones. We were interrupted by a girl sitting in the office who had been sent there by her teacher for something she had done. She was miffed. "How come the boys always get to do this stuff? Girls could do it!"

The teacher said, "I'll get the boys."

I said "Wait a minute, have you got girls strong enough to haul this stuff in? It's heavy..."

The girl was adamant that her friends could handle it. The staffer said, "Maybe another time."

I had done several teen dances for a church and while everything seemed to be going well, the organizers wanted to know it if was, indeed, what the youth wanted. I drew up a questionnaire to have them fill out, covering everything from the music to the decorations. As we passed out the papers and pencils, I found it interesting that the boys would fill them out quickly and drop them in the box provided. The girls would gather in groups and decide how they should answer each question.

One of the questions was whether it was worth it to decorate the hall for special events like Hallowe'en and Valentine's, since the lights were out, and you could not see much of the work that had been done. I was surprised but heartened by the answer from the girls' side. They said, yes, decorations were important because it made them feel like they were not only expected, but welcome.

***   ***   ***

There came a call from an agent. One of his DJs was ill and could not go out. Could we do the job? We agreed on a price and headed out to the Legion Hall in St. Albert.

What a surprise! I knew the people we would be working for. They had not heard that we did dances. We had a great night with lots of compliments, but an awfully bad morning after.

The agent tried to scam me. He told me the client did not like my choice of music (he did not know that we played only by request). He said he was fining me and offered me an amount much lower than we had agreed on. He finally paid up when I offered to have the client call him and dispute his lying claims. The Mamas and the Papas hit song "Creeque Alley" was playing in my head. "Broke, busted, disgusted, agents can't be trusted..."

Not every dance was fun. Some were sad, like the wedding dance we played where nobody came. The couple was obviously not well off. Neither the wedding dress nor the groom's suit fit well, and he was wearing old black cloth running shoes. They had been married earlier and this was to be the reception. No speeches, just a dance and snacks. They had put out a tray of buns and various cold cuts of meat.

It turned out there was another wedding reception that night for a couple they knew, across town. A few people came to the hall, offering congratulations and a gift, and offered regrets they could not stay. We would find out later they all knew the other couple would be putting on a fantastic reception.

As we sat with them in the empty hall, David and I decided to not charge them and just call it a night. They were having none of it. They had saved for the dance and they were going to have one, even it if was just them on the dance floor. The bride and groom told us they were going to leave for a while, to take their little kids home and put the meat in the freezer, and then they would be back.

While they were gone, we still agreed we could not charge them, and would play just a short dance and then wrap it up.

As we waited, the door opened. A man came in and looked around. "Where are they?" he asked.

I explained the situation and he explained that everybody was at the other reception.

He admitted he was the groom's brother.

I asked why his family was not at this reception.

"Because we don't like him, that's why. We don't like the way they live."

I asked what the problem was.

"They work for minimum wage like the rest of us, and they do things they have no right to do."

"Like what?"

He started to sound frustrated. "They, they went to Hawaii last year. Can you believe that? Hawaii!"

"So, what's the problem?"

"The rest of us can't afford to go there. Who do they think they are?"

I asked how they managed to go on such a trip.

"We asked, too," he replied. "They said they had been saving for a couple of years. Nickels and dimes and pennies. They bought no new clothes. They said they were careful buying food, and they found an extra job and never said no to overtime... and... and..."

He was looking upset. As someone who believed in setting and achieving goals, I was starting to admire them.

Then the door opened, and the bride and groom were back. The upset brother disappeared out a side door.

They went to the middle of the dance floor and we played the opening waltz. After it was over, the groom said, "We've been to your dances. You always play by request, so we'll just keep calling out the next song. We've always wanted to be able to dance to the songs only *we* like."

This went on for a couple of hours, and then they decided to have the last waltz.

As we were packing up, they approached us, carrying a paper bag. We wished them well in their wedding and told them this dance was our gift to them. There would be no charge.

They told us very politely they could pay their own way and did not want to be considered a charity case. They would pay us the agreed price. They put the heavy-looking paper bag on the table.

As they left, we opened it. There were a few bills, but mostly pennies, nickels, dimes and quarters.

I have often wondered what became of them.

***   ***   ***

We were at the Petroleum Club playing a dance for hospital emergency and other workers, and it was going very well. We were playing totally by request and the floor was full. It was time for a slow song, and although it had not been requested, we had a song that always filled the dance floor.

We changed the lighting and eased into Eric Clapton's hit song, "Tears in Heaven." It was written after the death of his son Conor, who was just four years young.

To our surprise, people started leaving the dance floor. A few started dancing and then stopped for a moment, put their arms down, seemed to have a brief conversation and then left the floor.

We had an empty dance floor. What was going on?

A woman came onto the stage and said, quietly, "You may not know this. We are hospital workers and we've attended several funerals of children we have known, lately. We've heard this song at those funerals and it's just not something we can dance to. Would you mind playing something else?"

We faded into a different tune.

***   ***   ***

We played several dances at Fort Edmonton Park and all went well, except one.

It started out beautifully on the second floor of Egge's Barn. It was a Christmas dance, and no cars were allowed near the building. From the second floor you could see why. With all the old buildings lit up and the roads and trees covered in snow, it looked like a giant Christmas card. There were no tire tracks.

Someone at the park had done a great job of thinking this through.

Then, something special: they were giving the patrons rides in horse-drawn sleighs – now it *really* looked like a Christmas card! The smiles on the people's faces and the jingling bells were wonderful.

The dance was for a group of hospital and related workers, and at the beginning, one of the speakers talked about how stressful things had been lately and the challenges they had faced. All nodded somberly at his comments. He perked them up with some great comments about their successes and urged them to have a good time, and "Don't worry about having too much to drink – we'll have taxis to get you home!"

Sounded like a plan to me. The party began and the drinks began to flow, and the floor was still full after a couple of hours. That was always the measure of our success.

Then they started doing something we had only seen at weddings when the newlyweds were about to leave on their honeymoon.

There was a huge crowd on the floor, some without partners, and they seemed to be crushing in on a couple in the center of the floor, or maybe it was just one person. It was hard to tell because we were not on a stage.

Then, above the music, a man on the dance floor started shouting "NO - STOP THAT! ENOUGH!" As we strained to see through the dancers to try to see what was happening, the crowd began to loosen up and move away from the center.

A man was storming off the dance floor, seeming to have anger in every step. A woman was trying to reason with him, but he brushed her aside and sat down, a mad look on his face.

As the music faded from a wild party song to something slower and hopefully, more calming, we heard the woman say just above the music, "Oh, come on, doctor. We're *all nurses*."

I didn't ask.

The fellow in charge wisely started collecting from people for a sleigh ride. The rest of the dance went off without a hitch, unless you count the one on the sleigh.

Pay to play!

We agreed to play a wedding dance at the old Provincial Museum. Then I got a call from the museum advising me that I would have to pay a fee to play there. I had never heard of such a thing.

It was explained that if I were making money there, I would have to pay for the privilege.

I asked how that could be, when the place had been rented by the wedding couple. Weren't they paying for the use of the place? No matter, I would have to pay. Not just me, but the caterer and anyone else providing a service. When we arrived to load in the equipment, we were told we could not use the front door, which was closest to where we were playing; we would have to go to the far end, where deliveries were made. That

would mean a long haul and several trips to get to the reception. Now, I was even more unhappy.

However, when we pulled up at the delivery door, a crew was waiting inside to unload and carry our equipment. That felt a little better, but not much.

At the reception, as the speeches were made, there were several Star Wars mentions describing various aspects of what this couple could expect from married life.

I had an idea, and as I looked at Dave, I could see he was thinking the same thing. We had a state-of-the-art mixer with a special pitch control. Dave would operate when I was speaking and could make me sound like a squirrel at the top end of the scale, or Darth Vader at the bottom. We quietly brought the bride over and explained it to her and gave her an idea of what she might say to anyone who thought she was just going to be an obedient housewife (there had been a statement from one speaker using a misquoted scripture reference). When her turn came, Dave turned her into Darth, and she made it plain she would have a say in what happened in their home. The guests loved it. I could not see the face of the groom.

Other DJs were unhappy about paying the museum fees to play there, and I made a call to the province about it. They told me someone had the contract to run the place and they could not interfere. A while later I got another call to play there. I told the bride there would be a surcharge to cover museum fees. She was surprised to hear that.

I suggested she call back and ask who else they were charging who might pass the added expense on to her. She called me back the next day. The reception was being moved to the Fantasyland Hotel.

Parental politics

We played several weddings at golf courses, where the vows were exchanged outside. We would provide the sound system for the actual ceremony, followed by the reception inside.

At one such event, we were cautioned not to invite the parents of the bride and groom to dance, because the parents of the bride were not there. The person told us they didn't think the groom was good enough for her.

We had learned earlier not to invite parents to do the second dance after the opening waltz without gathering information first. Too many were divorced and were not speaking, let alone dancing.

Bob and Dave at Santa Maria Goretti Hall

Deposition dance floor

Two lawyers were getting married, and since I had played a function for the bride in the past, we got the job. When she told me that she was getting married to another lawyer, I asked if it was someone I knew, since I spent so much time in the courtroom as a reporter.

She replied that he was from Toronto.

I asked which of them was moving and she said neither. They would maintain their practices and just take turns travelling to be together on weekends.

All went well until it came time for the opening dance. I always kept the curtains to the stage closed, so the guests were looking at the head table and not straying on to my equipment with the different types of lights.

As I announced the opening waltz, Dave opened the curtains, revealing the light show. The groom dropped his bride's hand and scurried over beside me.

"I see you have a mirror ball," he said, his eyes seeming to get big.

"Yes… of course."

"I hope you are not going to turn it on…."

I started explaining that I only turned it on for the slow dances, but sometimes not for the first one if the photographer asked me not to, because it might affect the pictures.

With a pleading look on his face, he said, "Please don't turn it on. Those things make me so dizzy… I… I might just… puke in your pocket!"

Then the bride came over to ask what the two of us were talking about. Her new husband pointed to the stage and said, "He's got a mirror ball."

She raised her eyebrows in a way that said, "So?"

He moved in close and started explaining something quietly in her ear.

The discussion seemed to be getting a little intense, and the looks on the faces of the guests showed they wondered what the two newlyweds were talking about.

Then the bride stepped back, and in a style that can only be described as "lawyerly" asked, "What else have you not disclosed to me?"

I decided it was time for me to step in, and I promised not to turn on the mirror ball, and they decided they'd best get the first dance under way.

For the rest of the evening, people came up to let Dave and me know, as politely as they could, that the mirror ball did not seem to be working. We were surprised at how many mentioned it. They had seen us at other weddings and liked the way we saved it for the slow, romantic songs. I indicated that there was an issue, and we were working on it.

The bride and groom had a car pick them up at midnight to take them away to their honeymoon spot, and as soon as the door closed behind them, Dave turned on the mirror ball.

What happened next came as a complete surprise.

The crowd applauded that the mirror ball was finally working.

Napoleonic nuptials

One of the most interesting weddings we have ever attended was on May 20, 2017, at the Princess Theatre on Whyte Avenue in Edmonton, where Courtney Pempeit married Steven Giebelhaus just below the big screen.

Photo by Samantha White/Navigo Photography

The audience may have had the most comfortable, soft, relaxing chairs ever seen at a wedding.

The reception was at the Southwood Community Hall, and I heard some guests saying it was the best wedding supper they had ever tasted. With preparation time given by several members of the family, they had created a buffet where we made our own tacos with more toppings than I had ever seen. Dessert – homemade cookies and soft ice cream.

And the wedding cake – everyone was talking about the wedding cake! The *wedding* cake was made of *pan* cakes. A stack of pancakes of various decreasing sizes. It was in honour of the bride's father, Dean Pempeit (who helped make it), who got up every Sunday morning to make pancakes for the kids.

Decorated with icing and berries, it was a fitting tribute.

As for what was on top of the cake, said Courtney, "I made the topper from a Harry Potter book. It is the shape of a necklace my mom gave me, that her mom gave her as a child."

As for why the wedding was at such an interesting venue, says Courtney, "When I was in high school, my best friend and I went to see the movie 'Napoleon Dynamite' at the Princess Theatre. I said to her, 'This would be the most amazing place to get married.' When we got engaged, we both agreed it would be perfect for us, as we love going to movies whenever we can."

As I write this, in 2021, a follow-up shows this Sunday morning pancake tradition still alive and well, starting with Steven making pancakes for his bride, and now their daughters love them, too.

Photo by Samantha White/Navigo Photography

It sure tasted good...

I thought I had seen about every problem that could arise at a wedding, and how to resolve many situations.

There was the reception where the caterer had not brought enough plates. They had called back to the office, but it was a heavy night, and they were all out. They rushed out to get paper plates, but the bride was not impressed, so they were walking around the banquet gathering up used plates and washing them as fast as they could.

There was the wedding where, even though there were plenty of bowls of food to pass around, kitchen staff came out with a special side dish and gave each person just one. It was delicious.

Later as we were packing up our DJ equipment, we could hear a loud conversation between the parents and someone in the kitchen when it came time to pay the bill. Turned out that the special side dish was expensive and was only supposed to be given to the people at the head table.

Our ballooning price...

At one wedding we learned an important lesson about how much to charge for our services. We thought we were charging a fair price until we went to set up at a reception where there were several balloons floating in the air from the centerpiece on every table.

On one of the tables was the bill for the balloons. I could not believe how expensive they were. The balloons cost more than we did. That would quickly change.

With this ring…

This next wedding started with a loud bang and a lesson in staying positive from the minister. It was being held in a large hall with a couple of huge side doors on a very windy day.

The hall had been beautifully decorated, and on each side of the minister was a large candelabra with three candles.

As the minister started the ceremony, someone, perhaps arriving late, instead of going around to the front door, opened the big side doors. The wind slammed the door open, and then whirled into the hall and tore down some decorations and attacked the candelabras, crashing both to the floor with the candles skittering off into the distance.

As you might expect, everyone was shocked. There were murmurs and moans and gasps, and some people were stepping forward to try and fix this wedding chaos.

I was impressed by the minister, who quickly surveyed the damage and the situation and immediately took charge.

Looking at the bride and groom, he said seriously, "If you two don't laugh about this right now – I'm not going to marry the two of you."

They laughed, although it may have been a little forced.

The minister invited them to have a seat while they got everything back in order and were ready to start over.

DJ disasters

Our sons Dave, Chris, and Kim also became DJs. Our daughter Katie also did a couple of dances.

They remember, as I do, that most dances went fine, with many thanks from the client afterwards, more bookings and even requests for an hour or more overtime.

But there were *those* moments.

Chris remembers (and this next group of stories are all from Chris):

"My very first gig out with Dad – I was 8 years old, and the roadie/librarian for the show – was a deaf persons' dance. They had some skits with props beforehand, which was very entertaining. Picture, if you will, a man with two hands on a shotgun prop, who then had to put the gun down to sign the words, 'This is a stickup...' and then pick the gun back up...

"Because they could not hear the music, the (hearing) person who hired us told us to lay the thousand-watt speakers on their face on the floor and turn the bass all the way up. He said the people would take off their shoes and dance to the vibrations in the floor. He handed us each ear plugs and suggested that if we wanted, we could play Michael Jackson's hit song "Billie Jean" many times. He said it had some of the best bass to dance to."

Sweet dreams

"At one wedding dance, I had everything all set up as required, provided the dinner and cocktail music, sat through the speeches, and was all set for the first dance. Everyone was waiting for the bride to return from freshening up in the ladies' room. Five minutes, ten minutes... fifteen... um, *twenty*... then one of the bridesmaids comes up to tell me that I can pack up and go home, and she hands me the cheque.

"Was it something I did? No. Trouble in paradise? No. Turns out the bride was narcoleptic, and had passed out in the bathroom, and wasn't waking up anytime soon.

"How do you tell the guests? Apparently, you just come right out with it. Not 'The bride isn't feeling well,' but 'Yeah, she's passed out, so, uh, drive safe.' I let the bridesmaid say it. You can't make this stuff up!"

Empty floor

"Then there was the biker wedding. Didn't know it until I got in to set up, but outside was a row of Harleys and an equally long row of guys in their leathers, vests with patches on, and beers in hand out in the parking lot. They wanted to know if I had some Zeppelin and Black Sabbath. I do, of course, so I figured this might be kind of a fun night. I love me some good rock and roll!

"Now it's time for the first dance. The bride is here, but where's the groom? Out in the parking lot with the boys. I'm sure not going to pressure him, but it's going on close to an hour we're waiting around for him. I suggest to the bride she might want to call him in. 'Dear, time to come in for the first dance...'

"'I don't dance.'

"Apparently, none of the other guys do either, so *all* the guys stayed out in the parking lot the whole night, the girls sat at tables talking, and nobody danced. It's tough when nobody's dancing. You're not sure if they hate you or not, and it makes it awkward when it's time to ask for the cheque. They told me they loved it though, 'And, thanks for the Zeppelin and Sabbath!'

"One of the many, many nights when all you can do is shrug and say, 'Well, I got *paid,* anyway...'"

Baby Bump

"The craziest one was a wedding where the bride was from a deeply religious background, and the groom was...um...not. The bride was pregnant, and her side was none too happy about it. Her family all sat, arms folded, looking daggers the whole evening while *his* family was dancing and partying with drinks in their hands. You could cut the tension in the air with a knife...especially during the speeches, when some of the groomsmen told sex jokes..."

Wrong Stage

"I once did a wedding where I made a very embarrassing error.

"I was at the Italian Cultural Center and got all set up on the stage in the big ballroom.

"Beautiful decorations on the walls. Nice big wedding cake. The guests arrive. I play cocktail music. Dinner is about halfway through when I get a frantic phone call. 'Where are you? You're supposed to be DJing my wedding right now!'

"I'm confused. Isn't that what I'm doing? Right now? Turns out that they had never specified in the contract what *room* in the Italian Cultural Center. I had assumed it would be the ballroom; I wasn't even aware that they even *had* other rooms to do dances in! 'Good news is, I'm *very* close by...'

"I had to pack up my gear and run it, piece by piece, down the hall to the correct room. What of the dance I was leaving behind? Turns out *their* DJ had skipped town with the money. They had paid in advance. They didn't know I wasn't their DJ, and I didn't know either. What are the odds? Luckily, the people who had hired me were very understanding, and the dance went great, minus the sweat that I had to keep mopping off my forehead in embarrassment.

"The other group, not so happy..."

Mosquito Mambo

"There was the dance out in the boonies in the summer, and the old hall had no air conditioning. Over 30 degrees outside. There were two doors on either side of the stage, so someone had decided to prop them open. Now, this is Alberta, mind you, so what do you get in the evening in the summer? There were so many mosquitoes, people on the dance floor were laughing their heads off at the sight of me, because I was in constant Kung-Fu mode. There wasn't more than a five-second interval (no, I'm not exaggerating) where I wasn't swatting or slapping at them. My very own dance move, for four hours straight – the Funky Mosquito! The light from my laptop was attracting them in droves since the rest of the stage was dark.

"The dancers came up and asked for overtime. First time I've ever turned it down..."

More puke

"Then there was the dance where you knew the *'We were so wasted'* stories were coming on Monday. Somebody had puked. And I mean *puked*. It was pink and chunky, and there was a lot of it. Right on the dance floor. Ever seen a buffalo poo? How they walk while doing it, so you get an elongated puddle? There you go. These people were so wasted, they were taking running starts at it, and seeing who could slide on it the longest. You would think it would stop when somebody fell in, but... no. The luge was the new event. *That's* something you don't see every day, people intentionally sliding on their bellies through a sea of vomit, even some of the girls in dresses. The fact that it was a wedding was the real head scratcher..."

Chris in 1990

Chris's Pickle Polka

"At my weddings, when the bride has thrown the bouquet and the garter has been caught, I then usually do a bit where I say the following: 'Ladies and gentlemen, we are going to find out why it is that _____ (whoever caught the garter) is still single.

Rumor is, it's the approach. Over here is the lovely _____ (whoever caught the bouquet.) Isn't she looking lovely, ladies and gentlemen?

"'Now, (garter guy), *this* is a *female*. What I want you to do is, you're going to walk over to her in your most *sexy*... your most *debonair*... the most *desirable* way you can think of and ask her to dance. Basically, what we want to see is your version of the mating dance. A little National Geographic/Wild Kingdom thing. We want to see a little butt shakin', right ladies and gentlemen? If we like what we see, we'll hoot and holler, but if you're not putting some effort in, we're going to boo until you give us what we want... Ready?'

"Now, 999 times out of 1000 this is all in fun, some drunk guy will shake his butt and do some lame dance while people video it for YouTube... except for the time that the guy (and this is no word of a lie) took off his pants. And his underwear. Yes, ladies and gentlemen, the best man is bare pickle in front of all of us. And shaking it, *really* shaking it for the crowd. What do you do at that point? I cut the music and hoped someone would cart him away.

"Of course, *now* when giving the instructions, I <u>do</u> specify no nudity, please... I felt bad for his cousin, though, who had caught the bouquet..."

The title has *love* in it

So, from DJ Chris, here's a tip. "If you want to request a song, it is *so* much easier to help you if you know what you want. Here are some not so helpful things I've had to deal with.

"'Play something good.' (No suggestions, mind you.)

"'Hey, I don't know what it's called, or who it's by, but they play it on the radio sometimes...' What station? They don't know. What genre? 'Uh, it's a slow song... goes like uh... I think... like... *something*... baby...' Now picture me rolling my eyes to myself, and let me tell you, it happens a LOT.

"'Ummm... I know it's got the word *love* in the title...'

"'Hey, can you play _____' (While I'm playing it.)

"'Hey, can you play _____' (I just finished playing it.)

"'Hey, do you have any (name of group)?'

"'Sure. What do you want to hear?'

"'Anything, doesn't matter.' Now, if it's a popular group, no problem. I can get away with whatever. If it's an obscure group that I know pretty much only that person and their partner will be dancing to, it's most irritating when they don't dance, or come up to tell you they don't like that one."

David remembers:

"There was the wedding at a rural community center. The groom wanted all heavy rock, but the bride wanted Top 40 pop and dance music. It didn't matter what I played, the friends of either would be up on stage demanding I shut that (expletive) off and play their genre.

"I finally had to get them both on stage and asked if they had ever travelled together and what they would listen to. They both said country music, but they didn't want that at the wedding. I had to explain to them that they would have to keep their friends at bay, and if they didn't like what was being played to just wait for 12 minutes and the music would change.

"Then there was the wedding at the Hotel MacDonald. The bride's playlist consisted of only Elton John and Radiohead. Those were the only two artists she would allow. People would come up telling me I was the worst DJ ever, and I would tell them that they would have to talk to the bride as she was totally in charge of what could be played. She eventually came up and told me I could play what was requested.

"After several occasions of brides providing total playlists of about 50 songs (many of which would be for listening, not dancing) we had to make it plain the bride and groom only got to choose the first three songs. The rest were for the guests to request."

Dave's Bridezilla

"The bride did not want cars at the rural hall so everyone could see her arrive in a horse drawn carriage. This meant that people had to shuttle others into the hall from parking elsewhere, so no cars were available. This turned into a big discussion as to where I would park. I finally convinced them to allow me to have my vehicle at the hall, provided I parked behind it, out of sight.

"Shortly into the dance, the bride decided to open some of the presents on the gift table. She demanded that the music be stopped, *right now*, in the middle of a song, because the gift opening was going to happen *right now* with everyone there. The bride took a chair into the middle of the dance floor and had the groom and best man bring her the table of presents so she could critique them as to whether they were acceptable.

"She opened one – it was a trip for two. She explained this was an acceptable gift. 'Very thoughtful. Thank you.'

"The next gift was a spice rack. 'Who the (expletive) do you think I am that I would want a spice rack? You obviously know nothing about me, or you would know that I do not cook. This is an unacceptable gift. I will leave it at the door, and whoever brought it can take it back and get me something more appropriate.'

"The guests were shocked. The look on their faces showed disbelief and then shock at what they had just heard.

"The spice rack was from her grandmother. The reception then turned into chaos and multiple people came storming over, grabbed their gifts and started to leave. The groom, the best man and a few others went to get their vehicles to give people rides to their cars.

"Everyone left the hall except for the bride, who then told me that she had to pee, and since I was the only one in the hall, that I would be holding her dress. I politely declined and she began to berate me.

"I ignored her and started to pack up. Finally, one of her friends came in, and was telling her off so loudly that I could hear the conversation coming all the way from the bathroom. "

I wonder if the bride and groom are still together.

Proud Canadians

"It was billed as a Canada Day Hockey Wedding. No suits and dresses - everyone was to wear a hockey jersey. Any team, it did not matter.

"As it turned out, it appeared all the bride's guests were in 'away' team (white) jerseys. All the groom's guests seemed to be 'home' team (dark) jerseys. A little bottle of maple syrup was at each place setting.

"It was announced that all the food was Canadian, they would be honeymooning in Canada, and that the music for the evening was also Canadian artists only. Indeed, the bride and groom entered the hall to the music of Stompin' Tom Connors.

"The 'Canadian music only' instruction lasted for about an hour and a half, until after several requests from their guests, the bride and groom said it was okay to play whatever the people wanted.

"We said we were changing it to 'Artists who *wished* they were Canadian.'"

Thank you, Dave and Chris for those unforgettable stories.

Side Hustle Karaoke

There came a time when we noticed at a couple of dances that some people were leaving early. I had taught my entertaining offspring to be careful in watching the dancers' body language to determine if they wanted a faster or slower song next, and we wondered why we were losing them.

The next time they started putting on their coats, I went over to ask if anything was wrong – was the music okay? It was. They were leaving to find a karaoke bar. Only one thing to do – we added a karaoke screen, and business picked up.

We had a groom kneel on the dance floor in front of his bride to sing her a song. We had groups come up to sing into our two microphones. It became so popular that at times it took over the dance, not always to the pleasure of the person who hired us.

We were hired to do a Christmas dance at a downtown hotel, and the manager of the company that booked us arrived and noticed the karaoke screen. He informed us that his company was classier than that, and that we were not to offer any karaoke tonight. We agreed to comply.

It was just after midnight that he lurched onto the stage, and he was drunk. He slobbered and slurred, "What are you waiting for? Everybody wants karaoke and I'll be doing the first song!" Then, "Have you got Frosty the Snowman?"

We had it, all right. It was in our children's section. No adult ever sang it. This guy sang it with words I had never heard before. A totally disgusting version.

I remembered hearing a comedian say once that although the Japanese had apologized for Pearl Harbour, they had still not said they were sorry for Karaoke.

Cute kids

It was a children's Christmas party and they wanted karaoke. Some of the older kids were good singers, and then a mom wanted her two little girls to sing a popular song. We gave each a microphone and put the words up on the screen. The music started and words started to roll. They smiled very sweetly as lots of pictures were taken, but they were not singing.

Trying to be helpful, I leaned in and whispered, "Sing the words on the screen."

One looked back at me and replied, "We're only four years old, we can't read."

Except for having pictures taken, I was wondering why they were both standing there so cute holding microphones.

Then the chorus came on and they sang it loud. Then, just silence until the chorus came on again. The chorus was the only part they knew.

Hotels
Chapter 3

As you visit a loved one in a senior's center and you see other elderly residents shuffling along on their walkers, do you ever wonder who they are or what they did in the decades before old age came upon them? You should ask, especially if they have no visitors. You might just hear a great story.

I wondered the same thing as I saw people happy about the Cromdale Hotel coming down. As we looked at the resulting empty space, I did some research and discovered an edition of the Real Estate Weekly from 2004. It contains a wonderful article entitled "The Rise and Fall of the Cromdale Hotel" by Lawrence Herzog.

Quoting, in part, from the Edmonton Journal, he describes a smart and snappy building that opened in 1954. It had well-appointed beverage rooms, a coffee shop, and a dining hall. Every hotel room had a telephone and wall to wall carpet.

This was the year television came to Edmonton and the Cromdale ordered one for every room. This venture was so successful they had to expand. Who could have known, as Herzog writes, that 50 years later it would be declared unfit to live in?

As with other businesses, the changing times brought other establishments with competing amenities and the client base would change.

I spend time regularly in city hotels, either speaking at conventions or doing a comedy show, or rolling in Layton Music (we had dropped Thunder and Lightning for a more adult crowd) for a wedding dance. I never played the Cromdale. The first hotel I worked in was in 1971, just after I came to 630 CHED. I got a one-night job playing bass in a pick-up band at the Strathcona Hotel on Whyte. We played for tips, and back then a $40 night was good money.

I asked the singer who hired us if she would be performing the next night, but she was off to Vancouver.

Gotcha!

As I emceed a wedding at the Holiday Inn, a fake wedding party sat down at the head table. I had been told this would happen and I introduced each of the people at the head table by the actual name of who was supposed to be sitting there. As guests, with strange looks on their faces, stared at their wedding invitations and then at each other, wondering how they all came to the wrong place, the real bridal party did a "gotcha" from the wings. Turned out the families of the bride and groom had been long known for playing practical jokes on each other.

New technology

At the then Coast Terrace Inn, it was our first night with wireless mics. At that time, there were only a few frequencies available. We were doing a Christmas party for Crystal Glass and we set up, only to discover another DJ somewhere in the hotel was on the same frequency and coming through our speakers. That was a shock. We changed frequencies.

DJs loved the then Coast Terrace Inn because the ballrooms were in the basement, and on a cold winter night, you could load in enjoying the warmth of the underground parking.

As I age and wait for my turn in a senior's center, those hotels are aging right along with me. It will be sad if I see a wrecking ball take out a place where I spent an enjoyable evening entertaining. I already hurt the day they demolished the Petroleum Club where we played so many weddings.

Public speaking

Chapter 4

I am fortunate to have the opportunity to do a lot of public speaking. One of the greatest challenges is when I am asked to speak on a topic that I am not totally familiar with, one that requires some research.

I got a call inviting me to speak in 2005, to a group of people who wanted to save the historic grain elevators. They were falling into disrepair and being torn down, and many people wanted these icons of the prairie saved. They had appealed to the province but did not feel they were being heard.

ALBERTA GRAIN ELEVATOR SOCIETY
ANNUAL CONFERENCE
SATURDAY- APRIL 23rd 2005

This Third Annual Meeting will be held in Stettler, Alta.
at the Royal Canadian Legion, 5010- 51st. Street.
Registration begins @ 9:00 am

The Conference is from 10:00 am to 3:00 pm
THEME: "Clean up your Act"

Panel discussion with the Experts on
Restoration and Painting
Fire Suppression Systems
Cleaning
Code

Opening Speaker: Garry Mar- Minister of Community Development
Luncheon Speaker: Bob Layton from 630 CHED & GLOBAL NEWS

Program courtesy AGES

I knew little about the history of grain elevators, and I always insist on telling an audience a story they have never heard before. I started asking around. Who can tell me a grain elevator story?

The answer was just a couple of blocks away, from my friend, the late Al "Bud" Wilson. He told me his own story about being told as a boy living in Gwynne, Alberta, to stay out of those elevators. People could suffocate in grain. But one day someone left a door unlocked and he went inside. He had been in it before with other people, including his older brothers Dave and Keith, and knew there was a lift inside designed to carry a grown man to the top of the elevator. To activate the lift, you just pulled on a rope and it engaged some type of mechanism.

With his brothers, he had been on the lift and then climbed up the ladders to the different levels where grain was directed by a lever to the various grain bins. The bins' insides were smooth and polished by the countless thousands of bushels of grain that flowed through every year. Inside, there was a ladder attached to a vertical wall and then to a floor sloped to about 45 degrees. There was another ladder attached to the sloped floor that stopped about six feet above the trap door. The ladders were so the elevator operator could have access to the bin to service the trap door and clean the bin.

Being curious, Bud told me how he crawled down the ladders and let himself slide on the highly polished slope towards the trap door. He did not realize that he would not be able to reach the ladder from the bottom of the slope. It was designed for an adult to use.

Bud was only eleven. He could not reach the ladder and could not climb up the slippery slope. He yelled and yelled, but elevators full of grain are great sound insulators and no one heard him. How could he get up that slope?

He told me he considered spitting on his hands and then wiping them on his bare feet to see if that would make them sticky enough to get some traction on that polished sloping floor, as he kept on yelling.

Then he heard one of his brothers on the top edge of the bin and got his attention. After a time, a rope was lowered, and he was able to climb out.

But then came another visit to that elevator. Someone had not locked a door and he ventured inside and over to the lift, which he decided to use by himself.

When I told this story in Stettler, the old-timers in the room said out loud, "No – don't pull on the rope – it's for a man, not a child!"

Well, Bud says, not knowing his brothers had operated the brake and put weights on the lift for counterbalance, he kicked the brake loose and the lift threw him to the top of the elevator. He could not stop it.

Allan "Bud Wilson 1934 -2012 Photo by Bradley Roberts.

So, there he was, stuck at the top. Without the proper counterweights, he could not pull himself down and had to climb all the way down on the ladders. No one else was at the elevator so he had to leave the lift at the top as he snuck out.

Later, finding the lift at the top, the elevator operator would have to climb all the way to the top on the ladders and then pull himself down on the lift.

Bud tells me there was a rumor around town that some kids had broken into the elevator and had been playing in there. They were all cautioned about how dangerous that could be.

Bud says he never went into that elevator again, mostly because of the big new padlock that had been installed.

The audience that was there to talk about and hear about saving the elevators liked my elevator story, but the best performance on that stage had already happened.

As Community Development Minister, MLA Gary Mar, Q.C., faced the audience about to speak, a woman in the crowd stood up, unannounced, and verbally tore a strip off him. I do not recall her exact words, but she was loud enough that she did not need a microphone for everyone in the room to hear her. It went something like this: "So, you came today. Do you even care about saving our elevators? I've written you several letters and did not even get the courtesy of a response! You totally ignored me! You can't even be bothered to return a phone call! I can hardly wait to hear what you've got to say for yourself." She concluded, "I am sorry if I'm being unreasonable." She sat down hard into her chair, to great applause.

Everyone's eyes shifted from her to Minister Mar.

As a newsman, I watch people, and like her, I was anxious to hear his response. It was something I will never forget.

He did not respond immediately. As I watched his face, I was sure I could hear the wheels going around. He thought for a moment, took a drink of his coffee, and then addressed the angry woman directly.

I do not have his exact eloquent words, but this is not far off as he spoke slowly and thoughtfully: "Madame, you say you are sorry for being, as you put it, unreasonable. There are two kinds of people in the world, reasonable and unreasonable. I've heard it said that so-called *reasonable* people do not often complain about their situation. They seem to prefer to adapt and make do with what they have, without causing a fuss about decisions that might affect them. Then, we have what some might call the *un*reasonable people. They demand accountability. They speak up for change. They work hard to make things better. It could be that unreasonable people are responsible for some of the great inventions in the world. I want to thank you for being, as you put it, unreasonable. You have every right to be unhappy. I do not know what became of your letters or phone calls. Over there is a member of my staff – please stand up so he knows who you are – give him your name and number and I can assure you your argument for saving the elevators will be heard."

He then gave the message he had prepared and headed for another appointment.

I called his office the next day, just to say how impressed I was with his response. From time to time, I call people personally when they have done something noteworthy. I often get the same response I got this time. His staffer did not know if he had ever received a congratulatory call in a situation like this before.

In April of 2020, Gary Mar, Q.C. was named president and CEO of the Canada West Foundation. As their website explains: The Canada West Foundation is a pan-western non-partisan think tank based in Calgary, Alberta. It primarily conducts research on issues of concern in Alberta, British Columbia, Saskatchewan, and Manitoba, but also on issues of national significance. The foundation emphasizes it has an evidence-based, non-partisan approach to research.

Gary Mar, Q.C.   Photo courtesy CWF

At the time of this writing, issues they are researching include public policy that focuses on prosperity in the west, in the hope that central and eastern Canada will see that, as Mr. Mar puts it, "What's good to the west of us is good for the rest of us." As he explains, "The diversity of the population in each province is considered a strength. Nationally, we must also consider the diversity in geography and resources. There is an energy difference between Alberta and Quebec, and public policy needs to recognize this diversity and ways we can benefit each other, if one sector is not doing well."

Kids' comments

You never know what to expect when you walk into a class of kindergarten or grade one kids.

In one instance, the teacher asked, "Who can tell Mr. Layton some of our rules?"

The answers came fast. "No pushing at the water fountain." "We all hold hands when we cross the street." "Take off your boots at the school door."

And the one I liked best, "Keep your little mudhooks out of the teacher's purse."

The teacher was upset when that one came out. I didn't know why. I thought it was a great rule.

Perspective

One of the most heartwarming introductions I ever had was at a Grade 1 class. My grandson, Braden, was in that class and had arranged with the teacher for me to speak. When I arrived, the teacher said, "Children, this is Mr. Layton, and he has a most important job in our community. Can anyone tell me what that is?"

A little girl put up her hand and said, "I know, I know! My mom listens to him read the news in the morning!"

The teacher said, "Yes, he reads the news, but that's not the most important thing he does in our community."

A little boy said, "He's on TV every night, and my dad always makes us be quiet. No one's allowed to talk while he's on."

The teacher said, "Yes, he does editorials, but that's not the most important thing he does."

At this point, I'm hoping she doesn't ask me what it is, because I have no idea where she's going. Finally, she says, "The most important thing Mr. Layton does in our community is this: He… is… a grandfather."

And, I thought, what a wise teacher. She put my life totally in perspective, for me, as well as for them.

But then, my life went sideways. After my discussion with the class, the teacher asked if I would like to come into the next room where the children had been working on something for a long time.

I went in. What a sight. It was a spaceship built entirely out of Lego and it must have taken a long time. It was huge.

As I admired it, I could see the children anxiously awaiting some approval. I knew it must be from a movie. Maybe Star Wars. Was it the Millennium Falcon? I had no idea – so, I asked, "What is this?"

Their little faces fell from anticipation to a frown, and they turned to look at Braden. He looked embarrassed. "Grandpa," he said very softly, as if he did not want the others to hear, "do you really not know what this is?"

"I just want to be sure," I replied. "I just want to get it right when I tell people about the incredible job you have done."

One of the other boys whispered to another, "Braden's grandpa does not know what this is..." The others looked at me and at Braden with sort of a *really?* etched on their little faces.

Finally, Braden had to own it. He took a deep breath and right in front of his friends he said, "OK, Grandpa, this... is... Lego."

A tasty talk

My first knowledge of the Lions Club came when I was little. I lived in Taber, in southern Alberta. A block from my house was a little park, and in that little park was a little wading pool. There was a sign nearby saying it had been provided by the Lions Club. As children we had no idea who the Lions were, or why they had built this pool. Did they just go around building pools for no reason, or was the reason that they cared about the children, and keeping us cool on a hot, summer day?

Decades later, as a newsman, I did some research and discovered the Lions Club was formed in Taber in 1934, and they did a lot more for the community than just build the wading pool I enjoyed so much.

Now, fast forward to the year 2000. I had done an editorial asking why Edmonton did not have a police helicopter, and donations were coming in.

I will never forget speaking at the Lions Club meeting at the Chateau Louis. I had been invited to speak there and receive a cheque for the police helicopter we were trying to buy. Their president used a white cane. As the guest speaker, it was my privilege to have him hold my arm as we walked along the buffet table. My task was to describe each food item in detail, and he would tell me if he wanted any of that.

As a newsman I've described everything from a fire to a funeral. Describing food is something else. As we returned with our plates, I told him I didn't mind helping with the selection, but if he turned out to have no teeth, I was not chewing it for him. That drew some big smiles.

Having the Lions Club aboard was a big boost. With them and the other service clubs, the bank account was growing.

I would be speaking at several other Lions Clubs.

From fiction to fact

I got a call from a school in Red Deer. They wanted to know if I would speak to students about the foolishness of smoking.

Then the person went on about how they would understand if I did not have time for them, given I was such an important person and all. I told the caller how I take out the garbage just like everyone else, but they seemed to be in awe that I would agree to come.

The caller started talking again about how important she thought I was to the community, and joking, I said I would have my private pilot bring me to the airport at Penhold and they could pick me up in a limo.

Program Director Wayne Bryant was in the newsroom when the call came and had heard what I said. We had flown together in the past in his plane, and he thought what I said was funny, so he offered to fly me down.

It meant a lot to me since he was my boss and knew I had been a member of the Calgary Flying Club. We landed at Penhold and he suddenly said, "Wait! Don't get out. Let me come around and open the door for you. We've got to play this for all it's worth."

Wayne, in upper management, was going to open the door for me? What was going on?

As he opened the door, I saw what he had seen from the sky while I was reviewing my notes: the just arriving luxury car.

The Fringe

I never thought I would ever perform at the Edmonton Fringe Festival, but the call came in 2019 when someone backed out of a show and I was called to see if I wanted to do one of my book talks – telling funny stories from my book *Welcome to Radio* and then selling copies of the book afterwards.

I was told it would be at the Hazeldean Hall and I wondered if that was really part of the Fringe, since it was far away from the main stages. I was assured that it was Stage 48, and we started advertising on Twitter, and Bruce Bowie gave it some mentions on his 630 CHED morning show.

I was surprised to walk into the hall. I had expected a typical community hall where I was used to speaking, but this one was set up with professional seating and lighting and sound, and a tech who knew what he was doing.

Hazeldean Hall was even set up with my choice of stages, lower or higher. I always prefer the lower stage where you can have more of a relationship with the audience.

Then, there was this opportunity:

Disability Day Committee
Presents
Keynote Speaker Bob Layton

BECOME ALL YOU CAN

Bob will share with us how he learned to see the person before the disability and the resulting change in his way of doing things. Bob will also show us examples of people with disabilities who have overcome great obstacles to find success in their lives. How do you become all that you can? Bob will show us some basic rules for settling goals and achieving them. And, he'll bring along some friends that will make you laugh.

WHEN
Saturday, November 24th, 2012
(12:00 – 2:00 pm)

WHERE
St. Paul Senior Citizen Center
4809 – 47th Street, St. Paul

And here is one of the friends I brought along. Al the alligator. He's from Florida, disguised as a pirate to hide from those who want to turn him into cowboy boots.

Wait until you hear how he claims he lost his eye.

Then there's Oz the ostrich. Had we been on stage during the pandemic, I might have changed his name to OztraZeneca.

Watchagonnabidfor'em?

Chapter 5

If keeping the mind active by learning new things, does, as some claim, help to ward off a stroke, maybe I can push back my senior citizen's calendar. Like other members of the Edmonton media, I am asked from time to time to emcee certain events. Or perhaps I'm at a function providing my DJ and Karaoke service, or doing my stand-up comedy routine and ventriloquist act, or some other side hustle.

Whatever it is, there may be a silent auction to raise money for charity, and we in the media get asked to do a live auction to boost the price of a couple of items. I've raised money auctioning for breast cancer; my only clue coming from LeRoy Van Dyke's "Auctioneer" song.

At a corporate party at the Old Timer's Cabin, I raised $1,500 for charity by auctioning off a Ryan Nugent-Hopkins jersey. (If you joke a lot, people forgive your lack of auction acumen.) Not being an actual auctioneer, I asked people why they were bidding so high, and they said, "Because it's Bob Layton asking!" While that is a gratifying response, deep inside I knew that I was more style than substance.

Then the bottom fell out – I was informed that in Alberta it was illegal for someone to take bids at a function and pronounce an item "sold" without being a qualified auctioneer. A check with Service Alberta found that to be true.

Then I got contracts for events that specifically called for a charity auction as part of the entertainment. I wondered: what do I do now? What if Service Alberta showed up at an event? I found the Auctioneering College of Canada right here in Edmonton, and I enrolled in the January course.

It was the best student/teacher ratio I have ever seen. Instructor Rick Wattie accepts only six students at a time and this course had only four. Imagine being told to chant by quarters (one, one'n a quarter – one'n a half, etc.) At the same time, other students are loudly counting by fives or tens. Now add the instructor throwing out random numbers to break your concentration.

Lectures covered everything from the illegality of an uncertified auctioneer taking bids (whoops) to the difference between auctioning real estate and chickens.

Part of the course was that before you could graduate, you had to do three live auctions in public. We were told we would be auctioning some food, by the can, so we had to learn the chant using nickels and dimes instead of dollars.

One thing I had to learn was what things were worth. As the four of us practiced by selling to each other, I pretended to buy a can of pumpkin pie filling for $5. Rick told me you could never get more than $1 and change for that item at auction. "Not even if you autographed it, Bob."

That night, as practicum students, we were taking bids at his public grocery auction. (At the time it was the last Friday of every month at 14912–128 Avenue in Edmonton). He started the auction and explained that his students, who were handing various cans up to him, would each do 15 minutes. I found a can of pumpkin pie filling and autographed it. He laughed, explained to the audience what had happened in class, and then started the bidding.

It went for more than five dollars.

He knew his business, but not mine.

Next, we went to do a public grocery auction at Carnwood Hall on Highway 39. He asked me to autograph a can of cranberry sauce and had *me* take the bids. How's that for putting a little pressure on a student?

It sold for about $15.

The lady who bought it stood up and said it would be displayed as a conversation piece and, "For that price, it should include a hug." A lady near the front stood up and said, "Yes, it certainly should!" That second lady was my wife, Marg, always supportive of my next project.

After doing three actual public auctions, it was off to Red Deer for more courses and auction law exams.

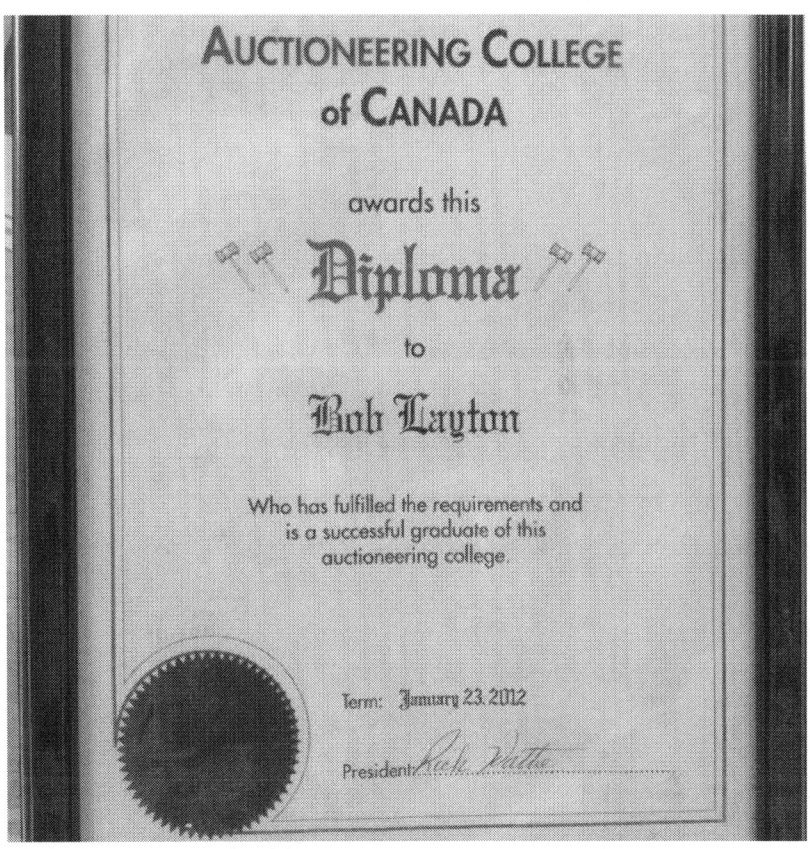

It was in February of 2018 that I wore my auctioneer's hat and raised some money for the Knights of Columbus and their charitable good works. I sold several sets of tickets for Oilers games and a couple of banquets to be put on by Chef Mario Nardelli.

To get in the mood for the night, I had attended an auction, where, among hundreds of other things, they were selling some small bits of Nazi memorabilia. As I sat there and watched, I hoped the buyers were bidding as collectors for historical purposes only, and not for any other reason.

After that they auctioned off some restaurant equipment. Bidding restauranteurs got great deals on everything from chafing dishes – the ones you see with the little flames underneath – to cutting boards three times as big as the ones you have at home. They even auctioned off the little metal racks that hold the jam and peanut butter on each table. The successful bidders smiled and were happy with the price, but all agreed with the auctioneer when he said we were all there because of the increasing minimum wage putting pressure on restaurants.

That's why we are here today," he said, "selling off everything from Chili's," as he put a food processor on the block.

It was about the same time I would add to my newscast a story about an auction sale in North Carolina. On offer was a paper cup Elvis Presley allegedly drank from in an outdoor performance back in 1956. It sold for more than $3,000, reportedly purchased by the owner of a classy hotel near London, England.

I wonder if this paper cup, featuring "The Coach" Jamie Herbison, Grant Weins, Bob Layton, Bruce Bowie, and Eileen Bell will be worth something one day:

630 CHED AM Stereo – seemed like a good idea in the 1980s.

Who said it best?

Chapter 6

As I write this, today is February 5, 2021. They have just announced the death of actor Christopher Plummer at 91. The Sound of Music was the first movie I took Marg to when we were dating in 1965. Yes, we were much younger then, enjoying what used to be the Calgary Stampede.

Christopher Plummer reportedly said after the filming something to the effect of, "Making a movie with Julie Andrews was like getting smacked over the head with a valentine." I can't imagine anyone saying it better.

Creative condolences

April of 2018 was a tragic time for our family. Three people died in one week. First, Marg's sister Vicki left this life, then my brother Kevin passed away, and then the angels came for Marg's Uncle Johnny.

Funerals would be in Calgary, Taber, and Medicine Hat, and I needed to arrange time off at work.

Newsrooms are known for dark humour. It may be the way we deal with tragedies the way they did on the TV show M*A*S*H. I once had a psychologist ask if any of us were suffering PTSD after repeatedly watching the 911 airline crashes and reading the story aloud over and over and over. No one had ever asked that before.

As I described the situation to my newsroom and hoping I could do enough creative shifting to cover all day parts, Eileen Bell said, "Hang on, let me get this straight. Your wife's sister dies, and then a couple of days later, your brother dies? Is that right?"

"Yes."

"That's the problem with the Layton family. You're so darn competitive!"

My brothers Ralph and Kirk had both been in radio, so the competitive line was not lost on them.

I told the story at my brother's funeral to some big smiles.

Photo courtesy Eileen Bell

I really enjoy Bluegrass and Country and Western music. For me, it's the way Willie Nelson describes it in his book, "A Long Story," saying this kind of music is often just "three chords and the truth."

Wednesday evenings were fun for me for as I sat in the Northern Alberta Bluegrass Circle at the Pleasantview Community Hall with my grand-daughter D'Ani. She had her Grade 8 from the Royal Conservatory of Music at the time, played piano and ukulele and guitar, and had come along to learn more about the mandolin.

I would ask her from time to time how she was liking it, since what we were being taught – just one song a night, in the simplest form – must have been way below her level of learning. She was grateful for the new musical things she was hearing, sitting in a circle of close to thirty people comprised of guitars, banjos, mandolins, fiddles, the main bass player, and me on my acoustic bass guitar. We always got there early to ensure a parking spot that would allow me to leave early, since I was up at 2 a.m., and we would set up the chairs in a big circle to prepare for the evening.

At every class, the excellent bluegrass instructor, Darcy Whiteside, would invite several people to come up and sing the various parts. This would mean finding the right key for them and then helping them hit the right notes for a particular harmony. D'Ani was new, and as he went around the circle looking for singers, he would always ask her, and she would politely decline. I knew she could sing. I had heard her play the ukulele and sing at church.

One night, the instructor was changing keys and explaining what the new notes would be, and when he got done, D'Ani gave herself away just a little. "If you're changing to that key, wouldn't the note be ___?" (I don't remember what the note was.)

The instructor explained it would be, except this was bluegrass and we were playing it the way the original was done way back in the day. Then he stared at her for a moment, some obvious questions in his mind.

One night, there was a song that had some tricky parts. He found two people willing to sing, but after going around the circle, he could not get the required third voice. Finally, D'Ani stood up, laid down her instrument and said quietly, "I'll do it."

After the song was done, he explained to the first two singers what notes they had missed and how to be better. Then he turned to D'Ani and paused. I was waiting to hear his instructions to her. There were none. He looked at her with a smile and said, "You have been holding out on me."

One night as we left it was dark, and as we got to my car a voice came out of the shadows. "Hey, Bob, would you like to buy some tickets to the Bluegrass Concert and Supper?" There, in the dark, I bought some. The seller was none other than the late, retired MLA and Alberta Legislature House Speaker, Gene

Zwozdesky, a lover of bluegrass who enjoyed playing the mandolin.

He had just arrived and was about to go inside to sell to the rest.

Gene Zwozdesky 1948-2019 Photo courtesy Zwozdesky family

I am writing this chapter two days before Gene Zwozdesky's funeral. When he passed, accolades were pouring in from all over, celebrating the love he had for so many different cultures.

As a newsman, I knew him in relation to politics, although from time to time he would call me at 630 CHED just to say hello or share a funny story.

Among those sending out messages of mourning were Ron Mercer, Bluegrass Circle President. For me he said it best, "Go rest high upon that mountain..." I will think of Gene every time I hear that song by Vince Gill. At the same time, I will be thinking of my brother Kevin. Kelliane Litchfield sang that song at his funeral, accompanied on guitar by Pat Layton.

One of the things said at Gene Zwozdesky's funeral was that no one can recall having a meeting with Gene when he didn't have a smile on his face. I would have to second that. And he put a smile on my face after a ventriloquist show.

I had just done a routine with my oversized squirrel singing the Ray Stevens hit, "Mississippi Squirrel Revival." Gene came over to my table with a big smile on his face and said, "You know, squirrels and rats are from the same family, Bob."

"Yes, that's true all right," I replied, laughing.

"So, why do you think it is," he asked, with a twinkle in his eye, "that people like squirrels but don't like rats?"

I told him I had no idea.

"Because," said Gene with a mischievous smile, "squirrels have better public relations people!"

Everyone at the table had a good laugh. Once again, he had nailed it with common sense.

What no one knew, until now, is that Gene and I had a project together on the side. He had called me to ask if I wanted to help write a song to honour CHQT's popular past morning man, Bob Bradburn.

"Zwoz," as we knew him, suggested we could do our own version of Bob's well-received, "This Week Had Seven Days," and offer to perform it at the next meeting of the Broadcaster's Club.

I had written some verses and sent them to him. He liked them and said he would start working on the music.

I was so looking forward to playing bass for Gene and whatever other musicians he would bring along.

Unfortunately, we would never make it to the stage. Waiting in the wings were some angels with an opening in the heavenly choir.

As I had explained to Gene, some people say my squirrel looks more like a beaver. That's because his father was a beaver.

He's a Canadian squirrel.

More on the ventriloquism later.

But first, Gene had more of an effect on bluegrass music than any of us in our particular circle may have known. As word got out that I was writing about Gene, I heard from Anna Somerville, president of the Blueberry Bluegrass Festival. She wanted to be a part of any tribute to him.

Logo courtesy BBF

Anna says, "I remember the night Gene Zwozdesky first entered the Bluegrass scene in Edmonton. It was on a Wednesday night in 2013 and he came rushing in to take part in our weekly jam with a briefcase in one hand, music stand in the other, and a mandolin slung over his shoulder. 'Who was this guy in the suit and high polished shoes, singing and playing so enthusiastically?' we wondered.

"It wasn't long before we realized Gene would have a big impact on bluegrass in Alberta.

"Very quickly, Gene made his way onto every bluegrass committee ranging from concerts to workshops. He joined the board of the Northern Bluegrass Circle Music Society and from there began developing relationships with the Foothills Bluegrass Club in Calgary. Soon, you could find Gene Zwozdesky behind the scenes at every concert or workshop held in Alberta. Everything about bluegrass was a fit for Gene.

"Despite his relatively recent introduction, Gene loved the music, loved the jamming, and he loved the friendly spirit of bluegrass. Watching Gene discover the music and community was a welcome reminder for many of us about just how special the genre is. There is a descriptive word that is fitting for bluegrass and for Gene Zwozdesky as a person, and that's collaboration.

"Gene made his biggest and most lasting impression on bluegrass in Canada when he got behind the re-launching of the Blueberry Bluegrass Festival in 2017. After 30 years, the largest bluegrass festival in Canada was shutting down after the Board had stepped down with no successors in place. Together Gene and Ron Mercer, president of the Northern Bluegrass Club, reached out to stakeholders with an interest in keeping the festival going.

"Gene chaired the meeting that helped elect me as new President. The newly formed Blueberry Bluegrass Festival had five months to produce a festival and the clock was ticking. His experience working with communities and unwavering confidence in the potential of the festival pushed us into action. The festival expanded by adding more stages and events aimed at creating an even more engaging festival atmosphere. When the town of Stony Plain presented the festival with the 2018 Award for Creative Excellence, Gene's comment was 'Let's go out there and get some more.' His confidence in our ability to present the largest bluegrass festival in Canada was inspiring. Blueberry went on to win the 2019 International Bluegrass Music Association Event of the Year.

"Gene seemed to be always rushing somewhere, but his enthusiasm for people and life experiences still made everyone feel like they mattered and was worth his time. You cannot say 'Gene Zwozdesky' at a bluegrass jam and not see a mixture of smiles and fond tears.

"It was a great pleasure to have met and worked with Gene. His memory will always be a blessing."

Anna Somerville – President of the Blueberry Bluegrass Festival

Run, Bob, Run...

We have always enjoyed eating at the Bubba Gump Shrimp Co. At the Ala Moana Center in Honolulu, we were prepared for a wonderful day. Marg and I were travelling with my brother Ralph and his wife Pat. We were dressed casual, but nice. Lunch at Bubba Gump's was going to be such a treat.

It was interesting to note that while the location was mostly a restaurant, they also had a section of Forrest Gump souvenirs.

As we enjoyed the open-air surroundings, the food arrived. Ralph reached for the ketchup, not realizing it had been exposed to the tropical Hawaiian sun. He struggled to unscrew the cap and had to hold it close to his chest to get a good grip. When the cap finally popped off, ketchup flew onto his shirt.

Our plans for the day did not include going all the way back to the hotel. Luckily, it was Bubba Gump to the rescue. First they offered their apologies, then asked Ralph to come to the souvenir shop to pick out a T-shirt at no charge.

The rest of the day was fun, and the shirt and the story behind it lasted for years.

When Bubba Gump opened in Edmonton, we were thrilled to go there. It was fun seeing the "Run, Forrest, Run" signs on the table. They were playing clips from the movie "Forrest Gump" on overhead screens. There was a "Forrest Gump" quiz for us to see how well we remembered the movie. I figured the staff would all have to be well-versed in the movie.

I was wrong.

We chatted with the server and she went away to get our order of various types of shrimp. When I saw her returning, I thought I'd have a little Forrest Gump fun with her. As we looked over the different types of shrimp, I slyly said to her, "You didn't eat some on the way over, did you?"

I thought she'd have a quick response like, "No, I only eat the chocolates," but instead she looked shocked that I would ask such a question.

I tried to explain it to her, but it was obvious she had never seen the movie.

Run, Bob, run…

Little fly…

I was trying to make some conversation with a new Canadian who spoke mainly Spanish. It was a hot summer evening, and as I smacked away another little flying blood sucker from my arm, I asked the fellow, "How do you say mosquito in Spanish?"

Whoops.

Coliseum Comedy

The Northlands Coliseum is now history.

Like you, I attended lots of concerts there and the one that still makes me smile happened on September 26, 1985 (and yes, I had to look up the date). It was the Dire Straits concert. It was a Thursday night and because of a previous commitment at a more formal event, I arrived wearing a three-piece suit.

Marg and I took our seats. In the row directly in front of us a young man was passing out little packets of something wrapped in tinfoil to his friends on either side. I wasn't sure what it was, and as a curious newsman I leaned over just a little for a closer look. He looked around at me.

"What do you have there?" I asked, simply wanting to educate myself.

He looked at me, then stood up and looked for a moment at my clothing. Then his eyes got big, and he shouted to his friends, "NARC!"

He and his friends did a very quick "Walk of Life" to the aisle. These "Sultans of Swing" or whatever they were using did not come back, so we had a much better view of the concert.

I sincerely hope they did not miss the show, otherwise they spent their ticket "Money for Nothing."

Sorry, sometimes I just can't help myself.

Silver Balls

Photo by Shane Blakely

When the shiny Talus Dome showed up next to Whitemud Drive in 2011, there were lots of questioning comments from you and me. People were calling the 630 CHED newsroom asking what the heck that was supposed to be. Perhaps if the city or the arts community had properly explained it before it arrived, it would have been better received. More people would have understood what it was supposed to represent. Some might even have been looking forward to it.

Some callers said it looked like the droppings of a great silver dinosaur. Many were concerned that this $600,000 piece of art came from a California artist and they wondered why a local artist did not benefit.

I was impressed with the response of the arts community to the disparaging remarks. They explained that good art should bring a reaction, either positive or negative. Their explanation made me feel better about some of the hateful responses I get to some of my editorials.

Then came the attacks on the Talus Dome that required repair and cleaning. I am on record as saying any of the positive or negative responses to the artwork should also be artful. That would not include the denting of the silver balls or throwing paint at them.

Physically attacking any sculpture or painting you don't like is like punching someone in the face during a debate because you can't think of a good verbal response.

Word play

The Oxford Dictionary's 2017 word of the year was "youthquake." It was reportedly chosen after a five hundred percent increase in the use of the term. It's not a new word.

Reading the story on-air, I explained how the editor of Vogue magazine coined it more than a half a century ago in describing cultural or political change brought about by young people. Today, we see it happening all around us in everything from elections to social inclusion to cannabis.

I wonder if the dictionary people might like to change the meaning of an old word the young people have seized upon for some reason. I'm referring to the word "amazing." The dictionary says it means, "astonishing, astounding, stunning, shocking, or breathtaking." Today those meanings have been watered down to become something you just like a lot.

In an editorial, I recounted how we hear "amazing" all day long used to describe everything from winter tires to babies to musicians to toys to diamonds and even snakes – you name it – the list is never ending.

How did that start? It's all part of the "youthquake."

Thank you!

Every year at Thanksgiving someone does a survey on what you are thankful for. I'm thankful for unseen heroes. You touch a wall switch, and a light comes on. You turn on the tap and there is water. We never see the people who make that happen.

I make a point to thank people who give me good service but sometimes it can cause unintended concern.

When my children were small, I had new brakes put in my van before a vacation. When I went to the service station to pick up my vehicle, I drove it around the block once to see how it felt. I came back and asked if I could speak to the mechanic who did the work.

"Is anything wrong?" they asked, looking a little concerned.

"No, it feels fine," I said. "Could I just speak with the mechanic?"

They looked very doubtful. "If everything is OK, then why do you want to speak with him?"

There were other customers now paying attention. Finally, they brought the mechanic out. He was wiping his hands on a brown cloth and looking like he expected to be chastised. I said, "Thank you for doing such good work and keeping my family safe."

It turned out no one had ever thanked him before.

Baptism by Blake

Marg and I were visiting Yvonne Woodruff, widow of my firefighter friend Keith. She was helping Marg by serging the edges of Joseph's "amazing Technicolor dreamcoat." Marg was making it for a play being put on by students of our drama-teacher son, Chris.

One of her grandchildren, nine-year old Blake, was telling me about getting baptized in a baptismal font. To add some perspective, I told him how I was baptized in a river.

He stepped back a bit and looked at me with an *oh really?* look on his face. "No, you weren't," he said with an incredulous tone.

"No – you were not baptized in a river…" He was not about to be fooled.

"Yes, I was really…" I was about to explain it was the Columbia River near Trail, BC, but he cut me off with "You were not baptized in a river – you are *not Jesus*."

I had hoped to give him a broader baptismal perspective, but this bright young man gave it right back to me.

Feeling old

I was speaking at an elementary school and telling the children how, when I was their age, television was not yet in people's homes. We never got one until I was 12, and it was only in black and white and had two channels. There was no such thing as a remote. You had to walk over to change the channel.

Some of them turned and looked at their teacher for confirmation. She nodded.

I continued, "Cell phones had not been invented yet. Seemingly shocked, they again turned to the teacher in unbelief to see if this was true. She nodded.

And then I said, "Credit cards had not yet been invented." This time, they took my word for it, but a little girl put up her hand, and in a sweet but worried sounding voice, asked, "Mr. Layton, if there were no credit cards, how did you buy food?"

Seems she had never seen her mom pay cash for groceries. Now... I felt old.

Menu Musings

This chapter is about who said it best. Sometimes you think you said it correctly, but someone else understood it in a different way.

Marg and I were at a McDonald's. I was standing before the cashier looking up at the selection of sandwiches on the huge, horizontal, brightly coloured menu above her.

We were going to have chicken sandwiches. I like mine crispy, or deep-fried. Marg prefers the grilled chicken which is not deep-fried.

I told the cashier we wanted one crispy chicken and one grilled, please, and a couple of drinks.

She asked if there was anything else, and I said, "No."

She asked, "Did you want anything else with the chicken?"

I said, "No, thank you." We had stopped eating fries, to improve our diet.

She gave us the number to wait for and we went to a table. When our number was called, and I walked over to the counter, I started to grin. I was absolutely surprised at what I saw on the tray, and was starting to laugh as I took it over to Marg.

"What is this?" she asked, with a questioning look on her face.

Laughing, I said, "I guess it's what she thought we were ordering."

On the tray were no sandwiches, just two pieces of chicken, all alone, except for each other. One crispy. One grilled.

As we were laughing at this, a gentleman who was obviously in management was walking by and asked if there was something wrong. We explained what had happened. He did not laugh. He hurried away to get some buns and the rest of the sandwich fixings.

At least they were grass-fed...

During the pandemic, of course, we started using the drive-throughs and had an interesting experience at A&W. I ordered two Teen Burgers®, one regular, one lettuce wrapped (I was trying to eat less bread). It showed up correctly on the big outside screen.

When I got home and we opened the package, both burgers had buns. There was no lettuce wrap. It was a busy time of day and I guessed it was easy for a staffer in a hurry to make a mistake. Just for fun, I sent a tweet explaining what had happened and how I would have to use my own lettuce.

I got a reply from A&W Canada. They wanted the location so they could deal with it. I chose not to give the workers any grief, but suggested the head office might want to wait for a different complaint, maybe one where someone arrives home to enjoy their hamburger and opens the bag to find it wrapped in lettuce.

Can you imagine the look on that face, especially if they had not noticed the lettuce wrap option in the corner of the menu?

Promotion?

There came a point during speaking engagements that I had to insist on giving the person introducing me a bio that I had written myself. More than once, the person giving the introduction had said they watched me every night on TV, but then gave the wrong station.

I carefully wrote that I was the News Manager. The next person selected to introduce me, seemed to be having trouble with her eyes. She would read a little, and then hold the script closer, then further away as she slowly read it. Then she announced I was the *new manager* at 630 CHED and GNR 880.

It brought a lot of congratulatory applause.

Props to your receptionist

I had read somewhere that your company receptionist is so important to people visiting your business for the first time that they should be known as the Vice President of First Impressions.

I had mentioned that at Corus in the front office. A few days later, look what was on the reception counter.

Do you offer your receptionist the same respect?

Have a seat...

Not only do you have to say it best, in a job interview you need to say it at the right time and sometimes in the right place.

I had an opening for a news anchor/reporter at 630 CHED and GNR 880 in April of 2019. A young man with several years news experience applied for the job. David Boles was working at CKRM in Regina. I liked his news delivery.

I was driving to an RTDNA convention in Saskatoon. My wife was along, and I knew she would want to spend an hour shopping at a quilt store. I asked if David would like to meet me in my car during that time.

He finished his on-air shift in Regina and drove to Saskatoon and found me in the parking lot. We had a most informative and beneficial side by side meeting.

A few days later, I hired him.

As David now recalls, "After the interview I drove back to Regina thinking what an interesting atmosphere that was. What followed would make me a better anchor and open the door to opportunities I never thought I'd have."

Travelling

Chapter 7

Marg and I were waiting for our flight to Victoria. We were sitting in the Edmonton International Airport in the WestJet holding area. It was not far from where Air Canada passengers were waiting.

The Arrival/Departure Board said Air Canada would leave first for Victoria, and WestJet would leave fifteen minutes later. Our pilot came running in, and asked the attendant if all the passengers had checked in. She said they had. He held up his hands and said, "Ladies and gentlemen, could I have your attention, please? We are supposed to leave after Air Canada, but since you're all here, if you'll pick up your stuff and we can quickly get to the plane, we can get off the ground first, and Air Canada can eat our smoke all the way to Victoria!"

So, we did!

Then we were on the runway, waiting to take off. The flight attendant was doing the safety thing. You know how it goes: the washrooms are over there, and the emergency exits are over there, and the floatation cushions are there, and here's how you fasten the seat belt. Since I know how to fasten a seat belt, I was looking out the window, watching the other planes. I suddenly realized she had stopped in mid-sentence, but I didn't care, I was looking out the window.

Then I felt a little hot breath on the back of my neck. I slowly turned around. She was face to face with me – this is true; I am not making this up – she says to me, "Sir, am I just not exciting enough for you?" She continued, "If you'll pay attention while I do it in English, Sir, you can look out the window when I'm doing it in French along with *everybody else*!"

I was impressed. I make a living giving deserving people shots, and she had just delivered a great shot at me. I considered it a work of art. After we got home, I thought I might make up a certificate awarding her the Best Shot of the Year. When I spoke with someone at the airline about how I might present it to her, they did not understand how good I thought it was. They thought I was displeased, and despite everything I said, when I broke off the conversation and left them, they were talking about giving me some free stuff or something like that.

Months later, Marg and I took another trip to the coast. I get up to go to work at 2 a.m., so I need to get to bed early. This flight should have gotten me back to Edmonton in good time, but there was a problem. Either they had changed something, or I was not paying attention when I booked it, because the flight was not coming directly to Edmonton, it was making what they called a "quick stop" on the way. (I think it might have been in Kelowna.) The "quick stop" took a little longer than it should, and time was dragging on. Passengers were checking their watches again and again.

Finally, we were in the air and up and over the Rockies. I could hear a little grumbling around me at the lateness of the hour. As we closed in on Edmonton, the flight attendant took the mic and hoped everyone had had an enjoyable trip. There was some more grumbling. She was very chipper as she said, "Thank you for flying WestJet." More grumbling and a little laughter. She started to say, "If you have any suggestions on how we can improve our service…" This time there was real laughter. She bravely carried on, "If you have any suggestions, please just keep them to yourself because we're tired too, and we just don't care anymore!"

The plane erupted in laughter. I thought it was a brilliant Public Relations move. She was clearly on the side of the passengers and they loved her for it. As we rose to collect our bags from the overhead, people were smiling and joking about what she had just said.

As we waited in line to deplane, we could hear snippets of what she was saying to the passengers reaching the door. "Please, you know I was only kidding, right? We really do care. We really do. I hope I didn't offend you…"

I know I was smiling broadly, thinking what I might say to her. Marg and I are often on the same wavelength and she gave me a little jab in the ribs and said, "Don't you dare be nasty to her!"

When I came my turn to hear her very sincere apology, I said, "Can you smell that?" She replied that she could not smell anything. I told her I could smell it.

"What do you smell?" she asked.

"Free stuff."

This was, of course, back in the day when WestJet was young and having some fun in the air. Hot Wheels cars would roar down the aisle when the plane was taking off and flight attendants would take the mic and do stand-up comedy. This was all long before they were forced into the real world of charging for baggage.

***   ***   ***

I saw a comedian once mocking the safety instructions on airplanes, especially about showing people how to use a seat belt. He wondered who these people were who didn't know how to use a seat belt. It seemed funny at first, but then I thought back to the time I thought I'd make some extra part-time money as a driving instructor, (yes, another side hustle) and I signed up for a driver instruction course with the AMA.

So, we were in the car, the instructor, me – learning how to instruct – and two students who would take turns driving. One of the students came accompanied by his mother, who told us he was new to Canada and did not understand a lot of English, but they needed him to learn to drive.

Our time was nearly up, and one of the students mentioned that other instructors would stop on the way back and let them get a milkshake. Our instructor said, "Okay, we don't want to get back late, so we'll use this as an example of proper braking technique. We'll pull into the parking lot of the restaurant, hit the brakes hard at 30 miles an hour, and then back off the brake just a second before we stop so everyone doesn't pitch forward. A nice, smooth stop." Then he said, "We'll have to be quick, so let's run from the car to the restaurant and then we'll have to hurry back."

So, he hit the brakes hard, let them off at the last second, and we threw open the doors and ran to get a milkshake. In the line-up, we realized there were only three of us. Someone pointed out there was still a fellow back in our car, and he was screaming. Screaming like he was about to die.

The instructor ran back to the car. The straggler was the new Canadian and he did not understand exactly what was happening. He was having difficulty undoing that seatbelt and what was worse, he thought the reason we had made a sudden stop and run for it was that we were under attack.

So, lesson learned: Some things we take for granted may not be understood by others.

A foot note

Could you describe your vacation in one word? For us, one word would be serendipitous, as we stumbled upon an item we didn't know we needed. My wife, Marg, had been having foot pain. We were driving to Vancouver and getting out of the car for a break was not pleasant for her. As we drove near Merritt, BC, she asked if maybe we could find a drugstore and get some of those Dr. Scholl's inserts you see advertised.

We went into a Pharmasave and Marg limped along looking for the Scholl's display. Unable to see one, she asked a pharmacist for directions and the woman came out from behind that high counter and asked why she needed them. I was surprised at that, but Marg explained, and the woman asked more questions and Marg explained some more. The woman suggested something else. She offered a ball about as big as a tennis ball with rubber spikes sticking out. She told Marg to put the ball on the floor of the car and roll her foot over it back and forth as I drove. Marg was doubtful but there was nothing else, so she bought them.

The first few miles were a little painful, but she kept rolling and then – the pain was gone!

Travel can be so educational.

Hope

We were packing for a cruise that would take us to the post-Mayan ruins at Tulum when the tour guide called our home. He said if we wanted to have a special experience, once our suitcases were packed, we should stuff every little corner with school supplies. Nothing big, just some pencils or erasers or crayons or little notebooks or whatever we could manage.

We did that and set off on our journey. On the way to the ruins, we passed some little houses where people were obviously living in poverty. Children would run out onto the highway waving pieces of pineapple they were hoping to sell to us. The driver did not stop but did slow down enough not to hit one of them.

There was also a fat rope that had been put across the road, maybe to slow us down.

On the way back from the ruins, the tour guide was peering out of the window at every little community we passed. All seemed to be in dire circumstances. I was feeling bad, looking at their poor living circumstances from the window of a tour bus probably worth more than the village. But that was about to change.

Finally, the tour guide pointed. "That one," he said to the driver. "Take us into that village. They seem to have a little school."

The driver was not pleased. He was supposed to take us back to the boat. These villages were not on the tour. The guide finally convinced him, and he reluctantly turned off the highway. Now we were on a dirt road and going down a hill towards this little community.

When the bus stopped at the edge of the village, we went outside and were handed our bag lunches. The place looked deserted. Not a soul anywhere. It was very strange. Then, a little face appeared around the side of a small house, then another, over there. They were probably wondering what our big bus was doing in their little village. These children just kept their distance and stared at us.

We held out apples and chocolate bars to them and they came a little closer but were cautious. We saw no adults. Finally, one child came close enough to get some food, then another, and then they all came.

They accepted the food but did not eat it. They ran back to their individual homes and left it there, coming back to gaze at their strange visitors.

How I wished I could speak their language.

The tour guide asked the driver to ask them why they were not in school. It was a holiday of some kind. The guide drew our attention to the cinder brick building that served as a school. All the grades would be in the same room.

There were no washrooms. There was a pit at one end of the school for the boys, and another on the other side for the girls. "The government," explained the guide, "does not help the schools. The only supplies these children have is whatever their parents can bring home, maybe some scrap paper and pencils."

The driver still wondered what we were doing there. All the adults were away during the day, working at various jobs. The tour guide told him to ask the children where their teacher was. They pointed to a little dwelling on the far side. "Tell them to go get her," said the guide. And to us, "Go get your stuff."

The teacher came slowly, not knowing what was about to happen. The tour guide told her we were there to help, and she and the children watched as the pile of school supplies of every kind got bigger and bigger. It was amazing how much people had packed into their bags.

She was so thankful for what we had brought and set the older children to work dividing the supplies into categories and bagging them up.

There were hugs and photos and much gratitude shown. We then took up a collection for an air conditioner since there was a power line to the school.

One of the people most affected by all of this was the bus driver who was overcome. He told us he had never seen anything like this. All the tourists he had bused around were consumers, who left behind huge piles of garbage.

We had come and changed things for the better, leaving behind things of great value to these children. He said, "Others leave trash. You left hope."

The people were noticeably quiet on the bus ride back to the ship.

It was probably the most fulfilling vacation we ever had.

Feeling hot, hot, hot!

On a summer trip in the US from Nashville to Branson, we were caught in a heat wave for days. The locals had tinfoil barriers propped up behind their windshield when they parked, but my rental did not, so even the steering wheel got hot when we left it to shop.

As we pulled into one small shopping center and headed for a little store to get something to drink, someone came out of that store with a big chunk of cardboard. He held it up to the door with one hand and with the other, he applied some tape across the top. Then he got out a black marking pen and wrote on it, "Air-Cond broken. Do not squeeze the chocolate bars." We wondered if maybe it was a local thing.

We went into the store and asked a clerk what number of sunblock they used. She replied that they did not use sunblock there. When I asked how they kept from getting burned by the sun, she replied that they did not go out in it.

Travel can be so educational.

There was a shop Marg wanted to visit a couple of blocks away and we thought we might walk it, keeping in the shade as much as possible.

We were quickly dehydrated.

Then, in the second block, a group of teenagers in blue T-shirts were standing on the sunbaked sidewalk beside a galvanized tub that was just having more ice poured into it to keep bottles of water cold.

They asked if we would like a bottle of water. I got out my wallet, but they said the water was free. Why would they be doing that?

They explained they were a Baptist youth group asking if they could please have the opportunity to bless the lives of others with something they stood in need of. I offered to at least give a donation, but they declined.

We accepted their blessing, with thanks.

Welcomed

So, when I told my friends I was headed to Branson, Missouri, for my annual country music fix (they do dozens of shows a day on the strip), there was a little concern. With what US President Donald Trump had been saying about Canadians taking a trade advantage of America, they were a little edgy about how we might be treated in what might be considered a redneck state.

Missouri depends on tourism for a large part of their income, and when I put my Alberta license plate number on the motel register, they were delighted to see us – the only Canadians there that day.

How Canadians were thought of would be an even deeper experience the next day at a country music show. It is traditional at an American show that part-way through they pause and give thanks for their soldiers and first responders.

They ask them to stand and be recognized with applause and an appropriate song.

This time it was different. While we were waiting in line, one of the singers, playing the part of George Jones, came out with his guitar and asked if we had any requests. I suggested "The Grand Tour." He launched into it and then asked where we were from.

During the show, after he had recognized their American heroes, he continued, "We also have some Canadians in our audience. Did you know that 30,000 Canadians fought in US uniforms in Vietnam, many in the US Marines and other special forces, for which they were given dual citizenship?"

Looking at us, he said, "We won't make you stand; we just want you to know how grateful we are."

I had personal knowledge of one who had served in Vietnam – he had applied to take a course at the Bob Layton School of Broadcasting – and being a newsman, when I got back home, I did some research to find out if his numbers were correct.

They were.

Food for thought…

We were driving through Westlock, Alberta, and we were hungry. Rather than pull into one of the usual fast-food places, we decided to look for something different.

There was one little restaurant, but we weren't sure if it was even open. It was in a plain, unremarkable building and the sign said Alberta Café.

We walked down to see if anything was happening there and figured it was probably a "burger and fries" place. If it was quick, that's all we were hoping for.

Were we ever wrong! When I opened the door, the delicious smell of Chinese food came wafting out. It drew us in.

The inside was also plain, but the buffet was wonderful and the people very friendly as they made a place for us at the long tables.

I had eaten at Westlock before, but it was at a banquet before a speaking engagement.

This was totally different.

We must never judge a book or a restaurant by its cover.

Travelling always involves food and not just food for the stomach – sometimes it's food for thought. On a road trip through British Columbia, heading for the coast, we were coming out of Kamloops on an uphill grade and careful to stay within the speed limit. It was apparent no one else was. We were on the inside lane, going as fast as the last sign allowed but cars were zipping past us at a much higher speed. Not just a few cars, *all* the cars, and they were way over the last posted speed limit. There were so many cars going so fast I could not get over into the right lane, which I assumed would be slower.

Suddenly, a car flew by us and then swerved across our front bumper and touched his brakes. I hit my brakes, afraid we were going to hit him, and he kept slowing down – taking us all the way down to 80 kilometers per hour.

What was he doing? We could have collided!

Then he put the pedal to the metal and took off.

At the same time, a new speed sign appeared – it was bigger than a regular speed sign and proclaimed the speed limit was now 120 kilometers per hour. I had no idea that speed limit even existed in the mountains, but happily joined the road race where others were mostly going 140.

We had not made any specific plans on this trip through BC. We were on vacation and would just drive until we got tired.

That happened at Blue River. I pulled into a motel but saw no restaurant nearby. I asked where the best food in Blue River was and was directed down a service road to a diner. I was assured I would find the best food there, and the information was correct. Our taco salads were better than we had enjoyed at home, and then I noticed a sign on the edge of the bar mirror advertising something called cabbage roll soup.

I like cabbage rolls, but I had never had them as a soup, so we surprised the waitress by saying we'd have that for dessert.

The food was great, but the surroundings not so much. I had noticed a stack of shingles on the roof ready to be installed. Good thing. The ceiling above us was apparently leaky.

It had a sheet of plastic and a hose and funnel to carry any rainwater away.

I arrived back in Edmonton to find quite a coincidence. Well-known 630 CHED and GNR 880 broadcaster Eileen Bell also stops at Blue River and enjoys a lamb dinner at the same diner.

She told me how she was having dinner when some bears showed up outside and started trying to open the lid on the garbage bin. Patrons were afraid the bears would come in and have them for dinner.

People feared these bears would just lean against the front door and it would easily open, putting the people on the bears' menu.

Photo courtesy Eileen Bell

There was a collective sigh of relief when the bears gave up and headed back to the woods.

The baddest part of town...

In March of 2014, it was a shock for Marg and me to see on TV the footage of the Chicago commuter train on the so-called Blue Line that jumped over the "bumping post" – sort of a metal blockade with a huge shock absorber behind it – at the O'Hare Airport stop, derailed onto the sidewalk, and then came to rest part way up the escalator. This was about three in the morning. News reports said more than 30 were injured, but no one had been killed.

A shock, because we had been on that very train and rode that very escalator just months before.

It had been vacation time, and we were busy trying to meet the three requirements we had for every vacation:

1. Go someplace we've never been.
2. Do something we've never done.
3. Eat something we've never tasted.

 That year it had been a bus tour that started in Atlanta, with a tour of the CNN complex. Getting into CNN was like getting onto an airplane. Security was tight. We had to empty our pockets and let them look in our bags and get looked up and down by staff with stern faces.

We visited many different studios and saw many different aspects of news gathering and delivering. It was probably more interesting to me than anyone else.

At the end of the tour, they took us to a tourist news studio, complete with camera and a teleprompter. "Who'd like to sit down and read the news?" he asked. "Your friends could video it... anyone? Imagine you, reading the news with a CNN backdrop..." There was some joking around among the people on the tour and then a couple decided to try it, stumbling along trying to read the teleprompter.

As they did that, my mind went back to the day Global Television, then known as ITV, was on the road to do the 6:00 news at NAIT. I was along to read the editorial, and when my turn came, Lynda Steele introduced me. As the teleprompter came on, it showed nothing but gibberish. My editorial had somehow become compromised. Lynda saw it at the same moment and jumped in with, "We have a technical problem, and we'll try to get Bob's editorial on a little later." She took a breath to go into the next story, and I jumped in with "It's okay, I was going to talk about..." and I ad-libbed the editorial I had rehearsed in my car a couple of times before going in.

Now, at CNN, Marg was giving me a little poke in the ribs. "Come on, do it," she coaxed. I didn't really want to. I was, after all, on vacation. But she persisted, and then others said, "Come on, it could be fun..." and the tour guide added his encouragement.

After I read the first two lines in my best "CHED style", people were looking at me and then Marg and asking, "Who is this guy? He's obviously done it before!"

Down on the bayou

One of our favorite TV shows is CSI: Miami. We were curious about what it was like to ride through the swamp in one of those flat-bottomed boats, powered by what looked like a big fan. We were told they were called airboats or bayou boats.

In Florida, waiting for a cruise, we looked for a swamp tour and carefully stepped aboard the boat along with some other visitors. I was sitting near the edge and dipped my fingers into the water. I wondered if it would be warm or cold.

"Get your hand out of the water!" shouted the guide. "This swamp is full of alligators."

We went for a ride and saw the alligators. The tour guide had a huge bag of marshmallows and did the alligators ever love those! He hoisted a chicken carcass on a stick to show us how high alligators could jump. I did not know they could jump several feet out of the water to get food. He showed us the spot where alligators had eaten a deer the night before. There was a 'gator sleeping on the bank that he told us had a belly full of venison and would not be eating for days. He proved his point by tossing it some marshmallows. It looked but did not move. Other alligators, however, scrambled in to get the tasty morsels.

Then it was down around another bend, looking for some young alligators, and they were right where he said they would be. He opened the marshmallow bag and their heads quickly raised in tasty anticipation. He tossed out a few and they were quickly gobbled up, but there were lots more marshmallows where those came from. He packed a whole bunch together like a huge snowball and threw the whole mess up onto the shore. A young one hurried over and tried to swallow the whole thing. That's when it got a little funny for some of us, and a little upsetting for others.

This little fellow had truly bitten off more than he could chew. After a couple of chomps, his jaws were tightly glued together. He shook his head back and forth, but his jaws were locked firmly in place, struggle as he would. Some of us were giggling, but others were decrying this terrible attack on one of nature's creatures. Someone else wondered aloud if we were about to spawn a whole generation of diabetic swamp creatures.

"I did it for the raccoons," explained the tour guide.

"Raccoons? What raccoons?" we asked.

"Watch the trees," he said. "Alligators eat raccoons, and those little bandits would like some marshmallows, too." He tossed more marshmallows up onto the shoreline.

Raccoons started to appear, cautiously at first. They looked longingly at the sweet treats and then over at the struggling alligator, and then dashed out to grab those tasty little white yum-yums.

The alligator was obviously upset. He lunged, closed-mouthed, at the raccoons, but they just quickly stepped aside and kept on munching. The alligator put his head in the water, swished his jaws back and forth and finally dissolved enough sugar to get his mouth unglued. The raccoons were watching carefully, and as the alligator came at them, jaws open this time, they deftly scooped up the remaining treats and disappeared into the woods, unscathed.

It was on the following bus trip that the music I loved would pop up at the oddest times. As we drove through Georgia we crossed the Chattahoochee River, and I had to hum the Alan Jackson song. Then it was the "Ode to Billie Joe" as we rode across the Tallahatchie Bridge in Mississippi.

Now, here we were in Chicago and a beautiful tour by night, ending in Chinatown. This was the end of the tour, for us. After we had booked, the company had added on a hotel for that night, and a day trip of Chicago for the next day, plus a ride to the airport. That information was never relayed to us as an option. We had already booked an early morning flight at O'Hare and had a hotel reservation at the airport as well.

So, now it was late at night and we needed to get our luggage off the bus and find a taxi to the airport. This trip had been great until the taxis wanted $150 for the ride. Apparently, it was a long way and there would be lots of traffic delays. There was no way I was shelling out $150.

We called the hotel, hoping they would have a shuttle service. They did not. We told them about the $150 cab fare, and they agreed that was a little high. They suggested that for about six dollars we could take the train, and while it might take an hour to get there, it would likely be quicker than the taxi. We were told to ride the Blue Line to the last stop, get on the escalator and follow the signs to the hotel.

We asked the tour guide. She thought we *should* be okay. She seemed a little tentative and you didn't have to be a newsman to pick up on that. I pressed further. We would have to take the Green Line from where we were, and then switch to the Blue Line to get to the airport. What made us nervous was that the Green Line ran through the south side of Chicago, and we'd all heard Jim Croce sing about the "baddest part of town."

Six dollars versus $150 sounded good, but... The tour guide switched to a more positive tone, now. She had lived in Chicago. Her advice: "Walk like you know where you are going. Don't start asking for directions, in fact, don't talk to anyone. Don't stand out."

Don't stand out? We would be dragging suitcases! The tour guide was coming full circle. Now she was *sure* we'd be all right. She would even go with us to the Green Line train station (just a block away) to get our tickets. As I looked at the map on the station wall, it appeared we would just be getting on the tail end of the Green Line and it did not look that far to the Blue Line station.

We got our tickets and took our suitcases on the elevator up to the platform. Try not to stand out. Try not to stand out. Try not to... are you kidding me? We're carrying suitcases. We are obviously tourists.

The train came and we got on the Green Line, now surrounded by people who had boarded somewhere along the route. The fellow across from us was passed out. Another was talking to himself. Others got on that looked like they must belong to a gang – my imagination was going crazy at this point.

I looked around. We were on an elevated train, the kind we'd only seen before on TV. The kind bad things happen on.

And then it happened. Two guys with guns got on. They looked each passenger up and down. They took a long look at us with suitcases and no hoodies. I looked from their guns up to their shoulder patches: Transit Police.

They rode with us to the end of the Green Line. They checked out every person who got on the train. At stations where no one got on, they got out and did a quick trip around the platform.

End of the Green. Time to walk to the Blue Line – we could see the signs.

We stood under the sign that said O'Hare, but we were alone. There were lots of people waiting for the trains on the other side, but no one else on the O'Hare side.

We waited and waited. The train on the other side was busy, but no train came on our side. We sat down on a bench. A woman approached us. She wore dreadlocks and had a guitar slung across her back.

"You're new in town," she said. "They're not using this track tonight, there's some problem down the line. You have to line up on the other side," she said, pointing to the crowd. "Or I can show you how to get to the front of the line."

There were lots of people around, so there seemed to be no harm as we followed her down the platform, up a flight of stairs, down another platform, and then down an elevator to where there was no crowd, and a train coming with the O'Hare designation.

It was a forty-five-minute uneventful ride, although I did note some taxicabs lined up at a level crossing as we went through. We came to the end of the line and took the escalator up to the hotel.

Being new to Chicago, I didn't even think to look back to see if the train was following us up those moving stairs.

Taxi lessons

Chapter 8

It was in the early 1960s that in a move to earn some extra money (yes, another side hustle), I got my Chauffeur's License and took a part-time job driving for Currie Taxi in Calgary. They would get a percentage of what I earned during the shift; the tips would be mine. The cars were older and well-worn, but it was a job. They were at the end of the Marda Loop. It was also the end of the city transit service. Soldiers who wanted to get back to Currie Barracks either walked or took a cab.

It was also the rule, as I understood it, that transit drivers were only to drive for four hours, and then they were to have a break from driving for four hours, and then get back behind the wheel of the big city bus. However, this was not how it worked out. They'd get out of the bus at the loop and walk over to the taxi stand, climb into a cab, and wait for the dispatcher to throw them a fare. After four hours as a cabbie, they'd get back onto the bus.

This was also about the time I discovered the drivers that got the best fares brought the dispatcher a "bottle of the finest" from time to time.

Many of my trips were taking seniors from Safeway home with their little bag of groceries. I always got out and opened the door for them, to which they would smile and say, "Fare and coffee!" That meant I was getting a ten-cent tip, which in 1962, was quite all right.

Then there was the time a teen-age girl was in the back seat coming from school, when she started making strange sounds and thrashing around. It looked like she was having convulsions. I pulled the cab over when it was finally safe to do so, driving with one eye on the road and the other on the rear-view mirror. I called the dispatcher to find out what I should do. "Oh, yeah, her," he replied. "Just keep on driving. It will pass. It's an epileptic fit." He sounded bored, which was a long way from where I was.

I was telling my taxi stories to a cousin who then told me how he got home to Bowness, on the outskirts of Calgary. The taxi there was also at the end of the transit line, but he couldn't always afford the fare, so he'd take the money out of his grocery budget. There was a Chinese food place near the taxi stand, so he'd go in there and order some food and ask to have it delivered, on the condition that he could ride home with the driver. He told me they never had a problem with that.

Once, I picked an older man up and drove a long distance to his home. When we arrived, he told me he had no money with him, but if I'd just wait, he'd go inside and get some. The older drivers had warned me never to fall for that, because I would never see the passenger again. I did what they suggested: I asked for some collateral. Problem was, he was not wearing any glasses I could keep and did not even have a watch I could hang onto. I asked him what he had in his pocket that I could keep for security.

Nothing.

Following what the other guys had suggested, I told him if he got out of this cab without giving me anything, I would have to call the police. He sighed. "Okay," he said reluctantly, "Hold out your ha-a-a-nd..." I did. He reached into his mouth and pulled out his false teeth and put the slimy mess right in my hand. I have never been so grossed out. He got out of the cab and was back in a flash with my money.

I made the best money during Stampede Week and got a great lesson. I took a flagged fare from the street and as we sat in traffic, one of the two men I had picked up, who was looking around the inside of the cab at the well-worn upholstery, asked what cab company this was. I told him. He said to his friend, "Make sure we never use this company. This car is a piece of junk." It was, but this was the first time I realized anybody cared. I didn't feel good about driving for them much after that.

DUI

Now, fast forward about 30 years. I'm at a News Directors convention in Saskatoon. I was on the way back to Edmonton, and the taxi driver taking me to the airport was making small talk. Suddenly, there was this beep-beep-beep sound seeming to come from the dashboard. The driver reached under the dash and brought out a thin, clear piece of tubing, the kind you would see in a home aquarium. He blew into it and the beeping stopped.

He put it away as if nothing had happened and resumed his conversation, but I stopped him in mid-sentence. "What was that?" I asked.

"Oh, nothing," he said with a wave of his hand. "It's just sort of personal."

"And I'm sort of a news reporter, and I want to know what that was." It took a little prodding, but he finally explained he had been caught driving while impaired in his own personal car. The judge was going to lift his license, but when he explained what he did for a living, the judge gave him an option. This sobriety testing equipment cost a good chunk of change to have installed and there were weekly rental payments, and it would go off at irregular intervals requiring an immediate response or the car would shut down.

He asked if I was OK with that. I told him I thought it was an excellent option, something I had never heard of before.

Attitude of gratitude

I was on the way to the airport in Edmonton. My cab driver was Black, and he had an interesting accent. When I asked where he was from, he told me where he had lived in Africa.

It was a snowy, bitterly cold day and as he drove carefully down the highway, to make some conversation, I asked him why he would leave warm Africa for cold Canada.

He told me he got asked that a lot. He asked me to look out the side window and tell him what I saw.

"Well, I see a ditch almost drifted over in snow and some fence, and that's about it."

"Nothing more?" he asked. "Look closer."

"Hmmm. I see the tips of weeds poking up through the snow, and there are some snowmobile tracks that are now disappearing in the snow."

"That's it? That's all you see."

"That's about it, yeah. What am I missing?"

"Look again. Look closely now. Do you see any children, dressed in rags and looking like they are starving to death?"

"Well... no..."

"Do you see any soldiers coming along to harass them?"

"Uh... of course not."

"And that is why I am here. I have a steady job and I am upgrading my education. My wife has a job, and together we have a safe home for our children who are in school."

There have been times when other immigrants have told me we have no idea how lucky we are to be in Canada. None had hit home as much as this graphic explanation.

I paid him for the ride and tipped him well for the lesson in gratitude.

"Hang Loose."
Chapter 9

For Marg and me, vacations are a time to experience the culture of the places we visit.

The cruise to Alaska was in the summertime, but it was chilly and rainy. In Ketchikan, not wanting to be confined to the indoors, we purchased jackets and went for a walk to see the sights of the gold rush days.

Later, back on the ship, it was still too dreary for some to be on deck, so nearly everyone went back inside. That left Marg and I and my brother, Ralph, and his wife, Pat, on the stern deck, bundled up against a light drizzle.

We were close to the shore and we could see what appeared to be an eagle at tree-top height. Looked like a bear in the trees. A sudden movement in the water revealed what looked like an otter with maybe a fish in his teeth. It was an experience reserved just for us. Something that said, Alaska!

The next morning at breakfast, as we looked at the menu for something different, some ladies at the next table did not like what they were seeing. "Are these eggs the only style you have?" they demanded.

The waiter explained that this was how the chef did eggs, to give people something different to experience on the cruise.

They were not impressed. "We want our eggs done the way they do them back home." Apparently, unlike us, they wanted something that said, Cleveland!

I wondered why they had come on vacation.

***   ***   ***

It was in Hawaii that I got some culture and a valuable life lesson. We were taking the bus, aptly named The Bus, from Honolulu to the north shore to visit the Polynesian Cultural Center.

The trip around the island to the PCC was interesting, as the driver stopped frequently to take on more surfers and arrange and re-arrange their colourful boards on the outside of the bus.

We were right behind the driver and the trip was taking longer than expected, and there were many more stops to make. The

PCC opened at eleven o'clock and we wanted to be there to experience the full day.

More stops. At one stop, with the bus now at standing room only, an elderly couple got on. There was no place for them to sit. Marg and I got up to offer them our seats, and some Japanese students farther back shouted at us, "No! No! You sit! You sit!" They gave the old folks their seats.

The bus was obviously running late, and I said as politely as I could to the driver, "Aren't we... uh... running... um... behind time?"

He turned to me with a smile, waggling his thumb and little finger in the Hawaiian "hang loose" tradition and said kindly, "Aren't you on vacation?"

Got it.

I felt like throwing my watch in the ocean.

And there was something else I learned about a vacation. With our schedule so different, there were things I did not think about, like taking my medication for high blood pressure. A couple of days had gone by before I suddenly remembered it as we were walking back to our motel. Those little pills were somewhere in an inside pocket of my suitcase. Now what? My doctor had told me to always remember to take them.

I noticed a walk-in clinic and went in. I asked if they could check my blood pressure. They did. It was normal.

I asked the nurse how that could be. "I'm supposed to be on medication to control it."

"Are you on vacation?" she asked. "Do you have a stressful job? I've seen this before."

Well, at the time, during certain parts of the day in radio we did have four deadlines an hour for live headlines and newscasts. And things could get a little tense when a story was breaking at the same time or someone called in sick, but I never really felt stressed, although others in my business had taken stress leave.

After the vacation, the pills were required again. It was in February of 2021, nearly two months after my retirement, that I would have a doctor's appointment that would start with a blood pressure test.

It was normal. Go figure.

The Eyes have it...
Chapter 10

In the early 1960s I enrolled in the Young Soldiers program. In a bid to get young men interested in a military career, the federal government paid us to train on weekends and during summer holidays with the regular forces.

Yes, another side hustle.

We were not actually *with* them, but we could see them as we went through the same basic training at Mewata Armouries and Currie Barracks, and the Palomino Gun Range near Calgary.

I had joined the Calgary Highlanders, the same regiment my father had been with during the war.

We mostly trained at Mewata Armories during the winter on weekends, and I became one of the highest paid Young Soldiers in Calgary. On top of the weapons and vehicle training, I discovered they paid even more if you wanted to come during the week to take highland dancing and to learn to play the bagpipes.

We were paid once a month. The Paymaster would have a table out on the Mewata parade square and names would be called out in alphabetical order and we would march to his table to be paid in cash. Invariably, when I would be called to march up, the Paymaster would question the amount beside my name, and look around for some clarification. I would have to stand there until someone came from the office to confirm the amount.

Everything military was always by the book, so it was a surprise on our very last payday, when the Paymaster started by calling up Private Zalzack, who always had to wait the longest. I'd love to see his story about that.

It was during summer holidays that we learned about camouflage. To this day, I remember the three basics were colour, shape, and movement. We thought stuffing twigs in our helmet netting and smearing mud on our faces was silly until we saw it from a distance. The twigs broke up the shape of the helmet and the mud kept our faces from showing up in the trees. Movement, well, that spoke for itself. It simply meant not moving a muscle when the enemy was nearby.

We boarded a deuce and a half (military jargon for a two-and-a-half-ton truck) and headed out onto the range. The instructor chose the side of a hill for our final exam. He told us to dig in and prepare the proper camouflage, and he'd be back in an hour or so to see if he could see us from the road at the base of the hill.

He did not come back, but a couple of truckloads of regulars did, coming back from a day of training. We knew they were out there, somewhere, because we could hear the explosions.

As we lay silent in our places, the trucks came to a halt at the bottom of our hill. A sergeant hopped out. "This looks like a good place. Set them up here," he ordered.

Some soldiers came part-way up our hill and drove some stakes into the ground, to which they attached some life-size cardboard soldier cut-outs.

Then they brought out what appeared to be Browning machine guns. We had fired those earlier.

The soldiers assumed the prone position on the ground and adjusted their guns, waiting for the command to fire. We were looking right down into those barrels. The young soldier taking a corporal's training course, who had been left in charge, looked very nervous.

We heard from the bottom of the hill a booming voice, "Ready, aim..."

Some of our boys jumped up, waving their arms, "No! No! Don't shoot – we're up here. We're doing a course!"

The real soldiers began to laugh. Some cursed. Our instructor stepped out of the cab of the lead truck shaking his head. "And you all just failed the course," he shouted. "Your camouflage of colour and shape was very good, but you forgot about movement, you (expletive deleted)! Get down here and get in a truck. We'll take you crybabies home to your mommies!"

"What were we supposed to do, sir?" pleaded one boy. "Let them shoot us?"

"It wouldn't have hurt much," he replied. "Even if they had fired, they were only using blanks to scare you."

Back at the barracks, as we stood to attention at the end of our beds, he gave us a lecture about following orders and told us again what ugly, horrible people we were. After he left and we were feeling like total failures, a corporal came around, and it seemed he was the "good cop" part of the team. He told us no one ever passed that part of the course, but we shouldn't worry, because our "camo" was good, and we'd all be rated as having passed. Then he told us to get some sleep because tomorrow morning was going to be challenging.

He was right. We rolled out of bed when the sergeant first came though and shouted at us. We were heading for the showers before breakfast, but he was blocking the door to the showers. "No showers," he roared. "And no breakfast until after your forced march. Full battle dress!"

It was to be a five-mile march before breakfast and our backpacks were heavy. At about the three-mile mark some were lagging behind, and a couple of them said they could not take another step, despite the profane urging of a sergeant who barked, "I am not going to take no for an answer from any of you young whippersnappers!"

Still, they were lagging behind and the camp was now in sight. We knew breakfast would be waiting, but some of us were having trouble putting one foot in front of the other.

Somewhere down the line behind us, we heard an officer shout, "Piper!" We heard the drone of the bagpipes starting up and then a highland marching tune.

The piper came striding past us and something magical happened. Now, our legs did not hurt as much. The backpack somehow became lighter. The rifle strap was no longer hurting my shoulder. Our spirits and our feet lifted as we marched to the piper's cadence.

As that was happening, the sergeant was barking orders, getting us formed into columns. "Left, right, left, right – straighten up that line down there, you (expletives deleted)! Swing those arms – swing those arms!"

We marched into camp to that piper's music and the sergeant's commands. With our columns straight and our arms swinging, we felt like we had just come from some glorious battlefield victory.

To this day, when I hear the bagpipes, I get just a little surge of adrenaline.

We learned to field strip and fire FN rifles and various machine guns. There was a live fire exercise where one group would be firing down the range and the rest of us would be monkey crawling in shallow trenches across that same range. We could hear the bullets whistling over our heads. It was a strange kind of rush.

We took part in mock battles with the regular soldiers. We dug foxholes in the pouring rain and fired many rounds of blank ammunition and set off coloured smoke bombs.

Then, as the rain got heavier, it got eerily quiet. Like they used to say in the movies, it was "too quiet." We used our ponchos to try to keep dry and posted our sentries, waiting for the attack from the regulars we were promised would come before daybreak.

It did not.

We saw some of them later at breakfast and asked why they hadn't attacked. "Are you kidding? It was raining. We don't go out in the rain." It was obvious they did not take us very seriously.

The rain stopped the next day and they did attack with smoke bombs and blanks.

Then we found ourselves in a mock-up of a town, learning how to enter a building, slamming through the door and rolling on the floor, weapon to the ready, as we made sure it was clear. We burst into one and cautiously made our way up a small flight of stairs. We peered out of the glassless window, looking for the enemy. We didn't see any, but our sergeant was in the yard urging us to jump from that window.

"Not going to happen!" one guy shouted as he raced for the stairs. He was part way down when the door opened and the sergeant growled, "I said *jump*!" He tossed in what some said was a tear gas canister and locked the door.

We jumped.

A couple of days later we were back on the parade square at Currie Barracks. We had heard the sergeant shout before, but never this loudly. In fact, he shouted so loud, his false teeth flew out of his mouth and landed on the parade square before us.

To say we lost it would have been an understatement. We were supposed to be standing "at attention." But we started to shake trying to hold in the laughter, and then someone started to snort, and that was even funnier, and then someone laughed out loud, and then we were all laughing out loud.

The sergeant's face was red with anger. He scooped up his false teeth and there was dirt on them. He turned his back, but we could see he was wiping them on his sleeve.

He turned back to us to try to regain his composure and our attention, but many were still giggling. Some were talking among themselves, something which was never allowed on the parade square when you were supposed to be "at attention."

He strode along, glaring at each of us. Some stopped laughing, some were still doing their best to hold it in.

He growled at others and then it was my turn. I could not wipe the big grin off my face.

"Private Layton, does your father *drink*?" he asked in a menacing tone.

Someone behind me giggled out loud. Someone who knew what everyone else out there, except the sergeant, knew. I came from a family of non-drinkers. They knew I did not drink because I did not partake when someone smuggled in a bottle.

"I said," repeated the sergeant, moving closer to me, "does... your... father... drink?"

"No, Sergeant!" I had finally gotten rid of the grin.

He looked smugly pleased with that answer. He backed off, and standing well to the front where everyone could see and hear him, he said, very deliberately, "Private Layton, if I was your father... *I* would drink!" Then he smiled, seemingly supremely pleased with his remark.

I could not help myself. The summer was nearly over. We would be leaving Currie Barracks in just a couple of days. What could he possibly do to me?

He now had his back to us, rocking back and forth just a little, enjoying his moment. The parade square was quiet. He was now back in command.

I took a deep breath. This had to come out exactly right. "Sergeant?" I said, in my most respectful tone.

"Why, Private Layton," he said in a most condescending manner. "What is it? Speak up, lad. Say it so everyone can hear you!"

"Sergeant," I said, "I'd just like to say that if you were my father, *I* would drink!"

Any semblance of order was now lost in gales of laughter, never to be regained.

I will not bother you with the new words I learned from him that day. The bottom line is that I would spend my last day at Currie Barracks, along with several others, enjoying the experience of peeling what seemed like hundreds of pounds of potatoes.

There were two vats to be filled. One was for the Officers' Mess, the other for the regular mess hall. Potatoes going to the Officers Mess had to be perfectly peeled, with every eye taken out. The others did not have to pass inspection, if you get my drift.

When the vats were full, a corporal came by, inspected the top row of the officer's potatoes only, and told us we were dismissed. He left.

As we reached for our jackets, the creative little devil on my shoulder whispered in my ear that we should stay for another five minutes.

That would be just enough time to exchange the top row of potatoes in each vat.

I decided not to do it.

Photo by Valerie Le Baron

The next day was the last day. We were told there would be a medical exam to make sure no one had been hurt during training, and some forms to fill out if we wanted to receive information on joining the regular forces.

We lined up outside the doctor's office and the guys seemed to get through the examination pretty fast. When it was my turn, the doctor had my form pretty much already filled out. "How are you feeling?" he asked.

"Uh, OK, I guess."

"You're feeling all right?"

"Yes."

He signed my form and tossed it in a basket. "NEXT!"

Next, we went to a room with lots of long tables and were told to sit down. There was a sign-up form and a pen at each place. The form was asking if I wanted to receive information on joining the military.

There were some regular soldiers helping with the forms and I asked one of the younger ones how he liked it. He said it was all right, provided you didn't mind being told when to get up and when to go to bed and what you're going to eat and when you can leave the base and when you can't.

A sergeant was now in the room. "Fill out your forms! When you're done, push them to the middle of the table and someone will pick them up!"

I was still thinking about it when the sergeant continued in a much louder voice. "Come on! Hurry up! We haven't got all day! Move it!

Some quickly signed their forms. I pushed my unsigned form to the middle of the table.

"When you're finished with your form, you are free to leave!" shouted the sergeant.

I did.

Despite my experiences as a "Saturday soldier," I grew up having the greatest of respect for those who served during the war I was born in, and those who would carry Canada's flag into the wars yet to come.

Keep your mouth shut...
Chapter 11

Logo courtesy IVS

I had played a lot of weddings over the years and had seen the same thing happen at many of them. The emcee would run out of material or speeches and would ask if anyone in the audience would like to come up and tell a story about the happy couple, or at least wish them well.

I would keep a low profile behind our music speakers about that time because I'd heard all too often what was coming next.

"Hey, Bob Layton's here – come on up and do an editorial about these newlyweds, Bob." And everyone would applaud.

At that point you're pretty much forced to go up, even though you don't even know the couple. Some of the bookings came from various agencies. I would go up and tell a couple of marriage jokes I had in reserve for the weddings I would emcee, but I never felt like it was enough. I wanted to do something that was completely different.

My A-ha! moment came at the 50th wedding anniversary of Marg's Uncle John and Aunt Irene Deering in Medicine Hat in 1997.

As I walked into the packed auditorium, the emcee said, "Oh, look who's here – Channel 33!" I did not even know they got my TV editorials in Medicine Hat.

This time it was legitimate when the emcee asked for any stories, because the hall was full of relatives and they had lots to say. At the end, the emcee asked if anyone wanted to sing a song or anything. Marg's brother, Hugh, was sitting at our table with his girlfriend. He playfully suggested they could go up on stage and he would sit in a chair and she could sit in his lap.

He would tap her on the back like she was a ventriloquist's puppet and they would tell some jokes.

She was having none of it.

On the drive home I remembered watching the old Ed Sullivan Show and all the great ventriloquists. I wondered whatever happened to Señor Wences and Topo Gigio and that talking head in the box – what was that all about? I remembered we sure laughed a lot.

Back home, I called an agent to ask if she had any ventriloquists in her roster. She did not, but was sure there would be work if any showed up.

Some rudimentary research turned up no place to take lessons in Canada. I ordered an inexpensive wooden "little boy" puppet and a correspondence course in ventriloquism from the US. I soon learned that spending time looking in a mirror trying to say the alphabet without moving your lips was not going to get me there.

My first actual lesson from a working ventriloquist came in Hawaii. We were there on vacation and had seen a poster advertising the ventriloquist in a hotel showroom. I went to find him before the show and offered to pay him to give me some lessons. Surprisingly, he declined the money, and said he would give me a lesson for free, during his show. He told me my assignment was to never take my eyes off him. I must never look at the puppet. Did I understand?

I said I could do that.

I was wrong. I found myself drawn to the puppet, which seemed to never stop moving. Whenever I caught myself, I'd look quickly back at the vent and he would shoot me a knowing look. Once he even smiled and pointed at me.

After the show he told me to never let my puppet stop moving. I was to sit it on the couch beside me when watching TV, and make sure it moved its head or shoulders exactly how my wife did. He said, "People never stop moving, and if you're going to create the illusion that this thing is real and can even talk, it's got to appear human as much as possible."

There was a ventriloquist ConVENTion coming up in Las Vegas and there would be classes for beginners. If you wanted to, you could even do Open Mic and some of the best would critique you when you were done.

I went.

My first lesson came when I tried to check in at the Imperial Palace, the ConVENTion site. The desk clerk looked at my reservation. I was getting the special ConVENTion rate.

"You can't do the checking in, sir; your little friend will have to do that."

As others in the line looked on, I got the puppet out and managed a "Hi, how are you doing?" It was about the only thing I could manage at that point without moving my lips. She checked us in.

The ConVENTion and classes went from early morning to late at night for two days. I was learning a lot. On the second day, after a long workout, the instructor said we were ready to try our skills out on the public. He told us the hotel would be OK with this since they were hosting the ConVENTion, and he told us to head out onto the gaming floor and have the puppet greet some people.

He sent me to work an elevator. So, there I was, my back to the elevator wall, waiting for the next people to come in. The door opened and I was faced with a group of very happy Japanese tourists, cameras in hand.

As luck would have it, I had taken some Japanese in university. I had the puppet bow and give them my best puppet-voice, "Ohayou-gozaimasu." To my great surprise, they bowed to the puppet and returned the greeting. Their cameras were flashing all the way to the next floor.

I was starting to learn, and their response started to build my confidence.

On the final day, it was time for Open Mic for beginners. There were hundreds of ventriloquists there from all over the world. Some had performed for us and they were fantastic. Some in my class opted out of the stage opportunity, fearing they would look foolish. I was there to learn, and no one there knew me, and I wanted the promised critique from a professional.

It was backstage that I learned an important lesson every emcee should know, but it seems none of them do. There were about a half a dozen of us lined up in the wings, waiting to do our five minutes. When the fellow ahead of me was on, the emcee came back to check on the pronunciation of my name, and then he measured my shoulder height against his. I wondered why he was doing that.

While he was thanking the previous performer and introducing me, he was adjusting the height of the microphone. When I walked up to it, it was perfect.

I got through my first public performance and was critiqued by a fellow who said he was performing at the Osmond Theatre in Branson, Missouri.

Back home, I was starting to do very short bits during our dances, just for fun. I certainly was not good enough to charge for any of this.

Then came the first paid ventriloquist booking. It was at the Palace Hotel. I was hoping it would be for a group that did not have high expectations. It turned out to be a meeting of doctors, who, to me, are about the smartest people in the world.

I did my routine, using some standard ventriloquist lines and a few of my own that got some laughs. Then, I had a falling out with the puppet, put him in his case, and pushed it way over to the far side of the stage. Using the *distant voice* technique I had learned in Vegas, the puppet asked for a drink of water.

The audience turned to look at the case. I could hardly believe it. Then they looked back at me for a reply, and when I said,

"No," they looked over at the case for the response. I was totally amazed. They were buying into this. It was a huge boost to my confidence.

Never one to stop learning, in the summer of 2013 I attended a ConVENTion and took workshops from Jeff Dunham and Terry Fator and became a member of the International Ventriloquist Society.

Terry taught us how he wrote comedy that he knew people would find funny, because they helped write it. He would supply a group of friends with pizza and beverages and suggest a situation and let them tell him what was funny about that. He was an excellent teacher.

Jeff Dunham told us about the failures he'd been through before he found the right puppets people could relate to and urged us not to give up if things didn't work out at first.

Bob with Terry Fator in a class on comedy writing.

Thanks to Johnny and Irene for inviting us to their anniversary, and thanks for the idea, Hugh.

While I appreciated the critiques from the professionals, I also learned some things from the audience.

During Reading Week, I was sitting on a chair in an elementary school library, and my puppet, sitting on my knee, was reading as the children sat on the floor in a semi-circle in front of me. Well, not all the children. A boy chose not to sit with them. He was further back, arms folded, with a stern look on his face.

The teacher asked him if anything was wrong and he replied, "I don't think the puppet is actually doing the talking."

I would love to know what or who he grew up to be.

In another classroom, the teacher had explained to me that most of the children responded when asked to come up and write something on the blackboard, but there were three who did not want to come forward.

She gave me their names and suggested I have the puppet invite them to come up. The first two smiled and came right up front.

The third one, however, looked scared. She put her hands on her face and scrunched down in her desk.

The teacher walked over and put her arm around her and asked what was wrong.

The little girl, peeking a little through her fingers, asked in a trembling voice, "How did the puppet know my name?"

The teacher explained and the student relaxed, but still did not want to come up to the blackboard.

It was not just children that had a problem. At one adult event I was into my routine when a woman in the audience suddenly stood up and pushed her way along the occupied seats and ran out of the room.

Her husband came to me after and explain that she was "freaked out" when the puppet looked her right in the eye. I explained that the puppet's head never stops moving and I control the eyes and never dwelt on one person. I was always scanning the room.

"Whatever," he said. "She felt he was looking right at her and it sent her off the deep end." He thought maybe it might have had to do with a movie she once saw, but he was not sure.

I offered to meet with her and apologize, but he thought that was probably not a good idea.

At the other end of the spectrum, after some shows, people come up and ask if they can have a picture taken with the puppet.

There were several times when I would bring out a puppet and I'd hear someone in the audience say to someone, "Oh, this is like what we used to watch on the Ed Sullivan show."

I was used to that, but not quite prepared for what happened at a banquet at Shaker's Acres, just outside of Edmonton, Alberta. I brought out the first puppet and was just getting into the routine when a table of mostly Indigenous people rose and started coming towards me. There were adults and youth. They came up quietly and sat down in front of me in a semi-circle, nodding at me, respectfully.

That threw me off for a bit, but I carried on and sometimes found myself playing to them more than the main seated audience.

When I finished they went back to their seats, but one of the adults came to see me at the end of the evening. I told him I wasn't sure what was happening when they came up. He explained they were teaching the young people to respect others, especially those who had something to show or teach them. He thought, since their table was part way down the hall, this might be a great opportunity to show them how to give their full attention.

Another lesson learned.

Bob and Uncle Henri Photo by Rob Hislop

Court stories

Chapter 12

I spent many years as a court reporter. I would read the news until nine a.m. and then be at the courthouse by ten for the latest on the stories we had been reporting on. When the court would recess for lunch, I would go home for my afternoon nap.

It was nearly lunch time and the judge kept glancing at the big clock on the wall and at the watch on his wrist. The defense was citing cases to limit the time his client would spend behind bars. The judge kept saying, "Yes, I know that one – what else have you got?"

The defense would start another one and get interrupted with the same thing. Finally, the judge said, "Look, in a situation like this I usually give (a certain number of months). Are you good with that?"

The defense agreed. The crown nodded. And the judge said, "Good, I've got a tee time in half an hour."

As the judge reached the bottom of the stairs and turned to open the door that would take him to his chamber, the convicted man said loudly, "You are a (expletive deleted)."

The judge froze for a second, then turned and faced the man. The judge looked at him for a moment, then at the clock. He looked back at the man. We were expecting him to be charged with contempt of court or something like that. We were wrong.

The judge said, "That… was just a lucky guess!" as he headed out the door.

Wormy meat

When lawyer Robert White, Q.C. was wrapping up a case, lawyers I had seen in other cases would come into the courtroom. I wondered if they were there just to observe and or maybe to learn. He was held in high regard by the court. There was one time during a trial over a death near Fort McMurray that he entered as evidence what he said was a scale model of the industrial plant where it happened.

The other side objected. "How do we know that is a model exactly to scale?" It was suggested some experts should have a look at it. The judge asked, "Mr. White, is this exactly to scale?"

White replied, "Yes, your Honour."

Said the judge to the other side, "Then let's not waste time. You know full well that if Mr. White says it is to scale, it's to scale."

Prosecutors were always looking for a way to trip him up. In one case I attended, a paper slipped out of Mr. White's hand and went slip-sliding through the air and landed in front of the prosecution table. White followed it and bent over to pick it up. I was close enough to hear the prosecutor say in a loud whisper, "Be careful, there. In my second profession, I am a proctologist."

White replied, "Oh? And what would be your first profession?"

In my favorite Robert White case, his client had two men accusing him of hiring them to commit a crime. We could hear the cell doors clang as they were brought out to testify. Their stories against his client were not consistent. There were some obvious differences we in the media section noticed.

White asked each man if he was telling the truth. Both said they were. White went through each man's criminal record and asked if they were truthful with police when they were arrested on each of the convictions they now had.

Each admitted they lied to police on the first charge, and then again a couple of years later when they were caught, and then again and again.

As best I can remember, the questioning went something like this:

"So, you've been lying all these years, but now you are telling the truth?"

"Yes."

"And when did you start telling the truth?"

"What do you mean?"

"You admit lying every time you've been taken into custody, but now you are telling the truth. When did this happen? When did you start telling the truth?"

During the closing summation to the jury, the prosecutor allowed that there were differences between the two men's accounts of what had happened but told the jury what was important here was that there was a thread of truth that ran through everything. Never mind things that were said that did not agree with the other man's testimony. He wanted the jury to convict on that thread.

Now it was White's turn to address the jury, and at first, it did not seem like he was even talking about the case. Instead, he talked about the weather.

This is my recollection of how it went:

"It's cold and snowy out there, and you've been sitting here for several days. Let's say your partner picks you up tonight and takes you to a restaurant. You want something warm and order a nice bowl of stew."

The jury was listening, intently, as they should.

"You bring out of the sauce a nice bit of meat. It is delicious. Then you spear a bit of carrot. Wonderful. Then you bring out a little piece of meat that tastes bad, and you take it out of your mouth. You can't swallow it. Your partner has not noticed, so you slide it under the edge of your plate and keep smiling. The next piece of meat is fine. But the next piece is green and has worms in it."

Some in the jury looked like they were going to gag.

"What do you do now?" asked White. "Do you keep putting things you can't swallow under the edge of your plate, or do you call the waiter and reject the entire stew?"

I thought it was brilliant. I used it as an example as I taught some beginning broadcasters about creative writing.

Photo courtesy Robert White, Q.C.

Well, it sounded good…

It was quite a catch for the police. A man had robbed a couple of banks in the same area and disappeared quickly, so they knew he had to live in a nearby apartment. They staked out several banks and finally made an arrest.

In court, it was a tragic tale. The man said he had not robbed those banks out of greed.

It was to help his dying little boy.

Reporters felt a tinge of understanding as we wrote about the child who needed medication to save his life, medication not available in Canada. There was an experimental drug out of Mexico that worked, but it was very expensive. He said that when he had enough money, he would order some and a doctor he refused to name would administer it.

It was all over now. He said that while he was in jail awaiting trial, the little boy died. He was prepared to take whatever punishment the courts deemed appropriate. The judge would need some time to determine how best to sentence him.

When the day came, the courtroom was packed. The judge started reading what felt like was going to be a lengthy judgement and we settled in for the wait.

A woman entered the courtroom, walked right down the aisle to the prisoner's box, which you cannot see into from the public gallery, and peered into it.

"It *is* you!" she exclaimed. "I heard your name on the radio but thought it was someone else with the same name – then someone said it was you, and…"

The judge demanded order and told her to leave the courtroom. She headed down the aisle, but in leaving, said, "He doesn't even *have* a son."

The judge and everyone else were shocked. Looking back and forth at the prosecution and defense, the judge said, "Did either of you check this out?" and then to the prosecution, "You might want to catch up with her, we're taking a break."

There was another adjournment while a really proper sentence was decided upon.

Get a lawyer!

The man was charged with smuggling drugs into Canada in a bedframe. He was in court with a bunch of his friends and being just oh, so cool in front of them. Asked how he pleaded, he smirked and said, "Guilty, your Honour," then he looked back at his friends with a "so what" look on his face.

The judge started explaining he needed a lawyer, but the smart aleck said he didn't want one. "Just give me the fine and I'll be on my way," he said, looking around for approval from his friends. They gave him a thumbs up.

The judge said firmly that he needed a lawyer. The fellow said firmly that he needed just to be fined.

"So," said the judge, "You are pleading guilty to smuggling drugs into Canada?"

"Yup."

"Do you want me to sentence you right now?"

"Yup."

"OK, seven years in prison. Take him into custody. Next case, please."

As the officers moved in and the fellow started sputtering, the judge said, "I haven't written it down yet. Did you want to get a lawyer?"

Yes, he did want to get a lawyer.

Proper dress

Us media types were sitting on a bench in the hallway of the old courthouse. Knowing better than to not look presentable, we were wearing shirts and ties. One fellow came in and joined us, asking questions about what was going to happen today and who would be on the stand. He was not dressed like us. His clothes looked like he had slept in them and he had a satchel over his shoulder with a long carry-strap. We made room for him as he explained he was an artist just hired by one of the TV stations to provide coloured drawings for the six o'clock news.

Just then a woman came along. I had noticed her talking with various people, especially those who appeared confused, and she seemed to be there to offer help to anyone who needed it. She bent down in front of the artist and asked if he needed any assistance.

He was taken aback. "What do you mean?"

"Do you have a lawyer?" she asked.

"What are you talking about?" He looked at us with a quizzical expression on his face.

She moved in closer and asked, quietly, "What are you charged with?"

We all started to laugh, and then explained to her who he was. She apologized and quickly moved on.

The artist gave us a hard look, and then said through his teeth, "None of you had better report this!"

But it was not over yet. During the court proceedings the judge appeared unhappy. "What is that irritating, scratching noise?" he demanded.

He got no answer. People were looking around.

"It sounds like someone scribbling on paper," he continued. Then, looking at the artist sitting near the front with the rest of us, he asked, "Is that you making all that noise?"

The artist nodded.

"Go sit at the back and hope I can't hear you!"

I was impressed with the drawings I saw on TV that night.

Catalytic crooks

One case I've been waiting to see as I write this book is the trial for those accused of stealing catalytic converters from vehicles.

Looking it up, so I could at least appear to know what I was talking about, I learned that catalytic converters are emissions devices located under vehicles. Their job is to take the harmful components in a vehicle's exhaust and render it harmless. This cuts down on the amount of pollution sent into the atmosphere.

Catalytic converters contain platinum and other precious metals that can be sold to junkyards, and that makes them a target for thieves, who can saw one off in just a few seconds.

Some people have had them stolen from their employer's parking lot while they were at work. One was stolen from a bus used by a seniors' residence to take them on outings. With the replacement cost close to $3,000, the seniors had to stay in their building until a kind company offered to replace it at no charge.

A car lot had eleven stolen. The owner, saying his deductible was $2,500, did not know if he could stay in business.

As I reported these stories day after day, I recalled a story my dad told me when I was just a boy growing up in Taber, Alberta. There had been a series of gasoline thefts from vehicles. I don't know if locking gas caps had been invented yet, but people were filling up in the afternoon and finding the tank empty the next morning.

My dad told me how one enterprising trucker, feeling sorry for the others, went down to the river and caught a rattlesnake. He brought it back into town and tied it around the middle with a piece of binder twine, fastening it to the truck's driveshaft with about a five-foot leash. He said the snake had struggled for a while and then seemed to give up.

In the middle of the night, they heard screaming and went outside to find a man with a gas can beside him screaming about how a snake had attacked him. They explained to him that there were no snakes in town, and then drove him to the hospital, where police were waiting.

When cars were being vandalized in my neighborhood, and things were being stolen, I told a police officer I had an old ghetto blaster in my garage. It looked impressive, but the cart players did not work anymore. I suggested I might have to leave it on the back seat of my car with the door unlocked, and the radio handle covered in Crazy Glue. He told me that if I did that, he would have to arrest me.

Police could tell by the footprints in the snow that it was young people and suggested we just not leave anything of value in the car.

I did have my CD collection in there, but I pulled my car up close to the house, thinking they would never be that brazen.

The next morning, it had been broken into and there were CDs thrown all over the inside of the car. I started collecting them and realized that not one had been taken. I guess they were not country music fans. They didn't even take the one entitled Greatest Banjo Hits.

It did not look like anything else was missing, but I had somehow forgotten what else was in the car.

A couple of days later I got a call from a woman who lives a few blocks away, asking if I was missing my Bible. Sure enough, I had left it in the back of the car, my name and phone number inside the front cover. Her car had been broken into and the thieves had left it in her car. I'm guessing they liked the nice leather case the scriptures were in and didn't bother to check the contents before they ran off.

Or maybe they opened it to Exodus 20:15, and were freaked out when they read, "Thou shalt not steal."

Conventions

Chapter 13

In my time as a member of the Radio Television News Directors Association that later became the Radio Television Digital News Association, I attended many conventions, literally from coast to coast.

Marg had come with me to Vancouver to see me accept an award, and during some free time, we decided to find some good Chinese food. I asked the locals and was directed to one that prepared some of the food right at your table. We'd never had that experience before, and we headed out. As we stood in the line-up to get in, we heard the person at the outside desk asking people if they had a reservation.

Our hearts sunk. With this line-up, there did not seem to be any chance of getting in. We had been to a restaurant at home in Edmonton where we were treated with disdain for not having a reservation. To this day we still say out loud the words the man at the desk said and the way he said it in such a disgusted tone, *"No… reservation."*

Only two tables were in use, but they seemed to reluctantly let us in, even though we had *no… reservation*. We were not that impressed with the food, either.

With this experience in mind, when our turn finally came in Vancouver and we were asked if we had a reservation, and I said, "Uh, no. Sorry. Maybe we'll come another time."

As we turned to go, the fellow said, "Wait – where are you folks from?"

"Edmonton."

"Edmonton?" With a big smile he said, "Come on in, Edmonton – we've been expecting you!!"

Someone escorted us not to the main dining hall where tables had been reserved, but to another huge area that looked every bit as nice and was filling up. The service and the food were absolutely excellent. I wish I had written down the name of the restaurant that made us feel so very welcome.

Jeans and T-shirts

The most unusual convention I attended was in St. John's, Newfoundland. Usually, you expect to dress high class for the final banquet. Not in Newfoundland.

They told us not to wear anything nice because we might spill something on it – we were invited to a "Kitchen Party."

I had never been to a kitchen party and it was quite an event, covering everything from the "Screeching in" ceremonies with the kissing of the cod to all kinds of drinks and delightful finger food that made you glad you were not wearing a tux.

Various bands stopped by to entertain us, all with great lyrics and some with home-made instruments.

Civic and provincial leaders came by to make us feel welcome.

At one point the emcee announced for those who were wondering about the food, "We do not eat salad here on The Rock!"

They also told the crowd the ice in their drinks came from the three icebergs they could see passing by the hotel window. They were called "Bergie bits."

I could attest to that. I was there. I had gone for an afternoon walk on the pier, and a fishing boat was offering rides around the icebergs, so I bought a ticket and climbed aboard.

There were a few other tourists and going across the harbor, it was as smooth as glass. Then we hit the ocean proper, and it was a whole different story. The boat seemed to be diving down - there were walls of water on each side. Then the boat would rise to the top of the waves and break to one side and start heading down again with those walls of water rising. To put it bluntly, people were terrified!

I was holding on to an outside corner of the cabin for dear life, afraid to let go, lest I get thrown into the water as the boat seemed to shift so quickly back and forth.

Now a lady was screaming. She was holding on tightly when the boat shifted. She had hit her head against the wall and was having trouble hanging on. "I want to go back!" she cried very loudly. The man with her also made it plain they wanted to go back, and right now.

The captain told them we could not go back until after we circled the icebergs, but that if it was so terrible, he would refund their money.

Then he put some music by Great Big Sea on the great big loudspeakers.

I had seen the captain walk by a half a dozen times as he circled the boat quite nonchalantly and not holding on to anything. I was holding on so tightly my hands were starting to ache. When he came around the next time, I asked, "How are you doing that – how are you keeping your balance? Is it just years of experience?" I tightened my grip – if that was even possible – as the boat began to rise again.

He said, "Do you really want to know?"

The newsman in me said, "Yes," although it may have been more of a squeak.

"Do you ski?" he asked.

"Some," I replied, wondering what that had to do with anything. I was not a great skier, and we were not on a mountain.

With a wall of water on each side, the boat was starting to rise as he said, "Let go and stand away from the cabin out here on the deck. Stand like you're skiing."

Was he kidding me? What if I fell on my head?

I let go, and nearly falling I caught my balance and stood with knees bent a little like I was skiing, but scared half to death.

"She's going to break to the right. You'll feel it coming – just prepare for a right turn but don't actually turn – ride the deck like it is your skis!"

Trembling, but leaning to the right, I started to get the feel. I was way more comfortable going down than I was going up, but how many times do you ski uphill?

Then I saw the captain doing something I had no intention of doing. He was leaning over the edge with what looked like a giant strainer. As we headed for the icebergs, he was gathering out of the water little pieces of ice he would sell to the bars. He said they were called "Bergie bits."

So, there I was, standing on the deck, shakily keeping my balance, and asking questions. He said we could sail around two of the icebergs, but not the third one. When I asked why not the third one, he replied that it was about to crack and could capsize us.

I looked at each iceberg. They all looked the same. I could see no difference. I asked how he knew the third one was about to split in half. He told me to look at the tops and tell him what I saw. Well, they all looked the same to me. The only difference was that birds were sitting on the two we went around, but not on the supposed splitter.

He said if the birds were not going near it, then neither were we. It would be too dangerous.

Deep inside, I wondered if that was his version of saying, "We're not going around it because I said so."

We were headed back to the harbor. I was feeling very comfortable standing and even walking on the rising and falling deck. In my mind I was now a sailor.

I was jolted out of my daydream by a thunderous cracking sound behind us.

I love cars...
Chapter 14

Marg and I on a date in my 1961 Chevy Impala "Warm and Windy"

I think my love of cars started in 1957. That's when everyone I knew in Taber was all excited about the new Chevy. It had *fins*. A group of us, just barely in our teens, went on a trek downtown. It was only several blocks, but we had to see this new car that looked so different from what our parents were driving.

One day there was a '57 Chevy at church and we wondered who was driving it. Then we discovered a brand-new Cadillac. It was black and had little fins. We cupped our hands around our eyes, pressed up to the driver's side window trying to see how glamorous the inside was.

Someone who came to church on a horse was also interested, and as he got close, something spooked the horse and it reared up. Spinning around, it started kicking out and put a dent on one of those Cadillac fins. We wondered where you would go to get something like that fixed.

My first car was a light blue Lloyd. It was a car produced after the Second World War, in Germany. Wikipedia says the name was eventually changed to Borgward.

I traded my Honda 50 motorbike for it.

My next car was a 1949 Ford 2-door. I had written on the side "Rockin' Little Angel." Then there was my 1961 Chevy Impala convertible. I named it for the first Chet Atkins song I sort of learned to play on the guitar. His song was called *"Windy and Warm*," but I changed it for my car to "Warm and Windy." I did not name my black Ford Mustang or the station wagon that would be needed after Marg and I married and needed room for the children.

And let's not forget about the Corvette all the guys were in love with after watching *Route 66* on TV, starring Martin Milner and George Maharis. My family had moved to Claresholm. My dad had a job in Calgary but could not afford the rent there, so we stayed in Claresholm while he saved up the money to buy a house. What I remember most about the Claresholm house is that there were two mice who used to come out and watch TV with us.

Word went out across Claresholm – at least, among the teenage boys – that there was a Corvette parked in front of the hotel on the highway that went through the middle of downtown. We hurried over for a look and stood around it, hoping the owner would come out, but it didn't happen.

The Corvette was magical to us, considering all the adventures those guys on black and white TV were having. No one even dreamed of having one. It was 1961 and a new Corvette would cost over $4,000, and I was making a nickel a frame setting pins in Al's Bowling Alley.

While I watched decades of Corvettes on the roads, my vehicles had to be practical to carry my family and groceries and music equipment and ventriloquist shows.

I couldn't even *consider* the Stingray I thought was so cool.

My brother, Ralph, and his wife, Pat, played the mandolin and guitar and sang great Bluegrass. I used to play a little bass with them. We were at the Blueberry Bluegrass Festival in Stony Plain, where we met the two Larrys who also played, Larry Seutter and Larry Roth.

It was a sad day, on April 9, 2017, when we learned that Larry Seutter had passed away. We attended his funeral, where the other Larry sang and the late Larry's daughter, Liz, spoke.

Liz told us that like every other young man, "His dream was to own a little fire engine red Corvette. But life happens and the dream was still alive and well, 45 years later."

Larry's widow, Anneliese, picked up the story from there.

"His goal was first to pay for and get the girls through University. He often spoke to me about how when that day would come, he would have some disposable income and was going to spend it on that dream car.

"Of course, I as a very supportive wife who appreciated all he sacrificed for his family, agreed with him every time he brought it up. But like most women, I had plans of my own for that disposable income. Besides, I had to share the money all those years while the girls were in school, and it was calling for new carpets and furniture.

"Many years had gone by and the girls were done school, and we decided a family vacation was in order. Larry, being an avid blue grasser, and our daughter, Liz, being a country music fan, we decided a trip to Nashville was in the cards, and it would be a vacation that would be enjoyed by all. We would fly into Nashville and work our way to Charlotte, North Carolina, and fly home from there.

"After a wonderful week at the Grand Ole Opry and seeing Vince Gill and the Time Jumpers, we headed out on the road working our way through the lush Tennessee hills enjoying the views and trusting the adventure Larry was taking us on. We hit the little town of Edmonton, Kentucky, population 1500, as part of the road trip, which was fun, as we lived in Edmonton, Alberta.

"Still no clue as to where we would end up, we continued our drive and as we were getting closer to Bowling Green, Kentucky, Larry remarked, 'While we are here, let's go and see if the Corvette Plant and Museum is open.' He'd heard the news in 2014 about a large sinkhole that occurred and damaged a bunch of the vintage corvettes in a viewing rotunda. He wanted to see what was left.

"As we went into the museum's foyer, there was a beautiful red carpet where they parked the cars decorated with a bow ribbon for the people who had ordered and were coming to pick up their new cars.

"It so happened that we were there just in time to experience a vehicle pick up. As the driver walked into the foyer, many of the employees of the museum and some from the plant would come out for the official key hand over. It was quite the fanfare as they applauded the new owner into the building, offered a glass of bubbly, took some photos, and then applauded them as they rolled their Corvette out of the building.

"They also had a few other cars in the foyer to entice the visitors to try and buy. Larry was like a kid in a candy shop. As I saw him walk up to one of the shiny new cars, his jacket flipped back exposing his cheque book in his shirt pocket, fear gripped my heart and I figured as soon as he sat in that Corvette, he was going to write a cheque for it and drive it home. And, all of this was going to happen quickly, without an opportunity for me to talk some sense into him. I cringed as he opened the door and lowered himself into the seat, holding the steering wheel in his hands, smelling the new leather, and touching all the bells and whistles that beautiful car had to offer."

Larry Seutter 1951-2017   Photo courtesy the Seutter family.

As Liz was walking around taking pictures of him in his dream machine, he quietly called her over and said to her, as Liz shared at the funeral, "I am so glad I got to sit in this car. It is the most uncomfortable vehicle I have ever sat in. I would not take it even if it were given to me!"

And, as Liz concluded, "Just like that, the dream of owning a Corvette was over."

After hearing this story, I went to a DJ I knew who'd had a couple of Corvettes, Jungle Jay. I told him the story and waited for his reaction. To my surprise, he agreed, "They are not all that comfortable."

"Then, why…" I started.

"Because they're really fast… and you know… everybody sort of… looks when you go by."

You can read a lot more about the car culture that existed at 630 CHED back in the day in my book, *Welcome to Radio*.

Plugged in

The extremely cold weather of February 2019 brought back memories of when 630 CHED was located downtown, and Eddie Keen did the editorials. One winter he bought an old Thunderbird. Most people I talk with agree it was probably a '63 or '64.

He had a new engine installed in it, and the next morning it would not start. The previous engine had been OK in the cold weather, he just wanted a new one. Eddie had something replaced, we think it was the battery, but the next morning it still would not start. Now it had to be towed and have something else replaced, maybe the starter, but again it would not start.

He was not happy. He told us how a friend of his son John would walk him to school every morning and was learning auto repair. He offered to have a look.

Eddie told us how the boy slid a piece of cardboard under the car in the snow and climbed on it for a look. He was only under there for a couple of seconds when he emerged to say, "Mr. Keen, that block heater cable wrapped around your grill that you plug in at night – it's not connected to anything. This engine has no block heater."

Eddie was not pleased as he told us that story. He was grimacing as he drummed his fingers on the desk and said, "I can't believe it. The block heater was missing, in a city like Edmonton!"

We laughed, just a little.

"Editorial, right?" we said.

"Yup."

Christmas

Chapter 15

Christmas 2017 was great being with family. Luckily, we were eating at my son Chris's place because on the one day of the year you cannot buy a refrigerator, ours quit after seven years.

Sour milk is not a good way to wake up.

On Boxing Day, I went to a big box store to buy a new refrigerator because everything was on sale. It was not as easy as I had expected. I was told that if I wanted to replace our "freezerless" fridge, or the *All-fridge* as it was called, because it was a specialty item, it would take two weeks to arrive. I tried another big box store with a packed parking lot, but they could not help, either.

Marg and I would have to decide if we could live without a fridge for two weeks or if we would have to settle for a standard fridge and freezer. Feeling a little desperate, we stopped at a small store that specialized in dented appliances.

To our surprise, they told us there was a freezerless fridge in their warehouse and they could deliver it the next day.

As we did the paperwork, the delivery crew arrived and said they could actually deliver it for us right now, if that was convenient. Convenient? Are you kidding? Right now, versus two weeks? We had it in the kitchen within two hours.

The lesson: Sometimes bigger isn't always better.

As I once heard a comedian say, I could hardly wait for Marg to open the new fridge door so I could see her face light up!

Here comes Santa Claus...

1971, the year I came to 630 CHED, was the same year another man named Bob first drove for 630 CHED Santas Anonymous. Like some others in the 1970s, he had longish hair, drove an old, loud car (a 1961 Pontiac Parisienne – just a little souped up) and even had a sheepskin coat.

When he heard the annual tear-jerking rendition of *A Creature Was Stirring*, and heard Jerry Forbes say, "Mommy, was that Jesus?" he was so touched he had to call and tell me about it.

When my book, *Welcome to Radio*, came out, he bought one copy out of the first one thousand printed. He got the only copy that was misassembled by the printer (that I know of).

He called to let me know, and I was so embarrassed I drove across the city to his house to replace it.

This year, 2018, for the 47th time, he was again in line to deliver toys. The line was cut off right in front of him.

What?

There were no more gifts to deliver.

How could that be?

He stood there, devastated, and could not bring himself to leave.

And then it happened (there I go with Jerry Forbes again): the lady who was the last to show her driver's license and insurance was told she could not deliver this year, because her insurance had expired. Bob went from deflated to elated in about a second, as he was asked to take her place.

It would be a very merry Christmas for Bob, as well as the children he would lovingly serve.

Then came the pandemic of 2020, and 630 CHED Santas Anonymous could not break public health safety rules by having people lined up inside the depot.

After much thought, the elves in charge decided the only way they could do a pandemic delivery safely for their staff and volunteers and the public was to have potential drivers call and book a time to drive up in their car for a curbside pick-up. Volunteers would bring the bags of toys from the depot to the waiting cars.

Included in that line-up was Bob Demers, who was booked for both days, taking the maximum number of bags allowed. This was his 49th year of service.

As Bob looks forward to his 50th anniversary of delivering next year, I think of the strange coincidence that caused our paths to cross and allowed his story to be told.

Things that make you go "Hmmmmm…."

Bob Demers

Photo courtesy Santas Anonymous

Speaking of coincidences

We had a most interesting weekend in 2019. On Hallowe'en I went with my wife Marg to pick up a box of chocolates from Purdys for her sister Wendy's 65th surprise birthday party.

It turned out to be a bigger surprise than anyone thought.

The box of chocolates Marg wanted the most was done up in Hallowe'en colours, including an orange ribbon, but the party was November 2nd, so that wouldn't do.

The lady at the till, in some of the best customer service we have experienced, was kind enough to redecorate the box to include a purple ribbon.

Perfect.

At the party, in Calgary, we all shouted, "Surprise!" and then we discovered this was a bittersweet time for her birthday. November 2nd was also the anniversary of the day her favorite aunt, Betty, had passed away. She had been so close to Aunt Betty and was feeling the pain of this anniversary.

As the party progressed, she was wondering where Betty was now. Was she in heaven? Is there even a heaven? If so, what would Betty be doing at this time as Wendy was enjoying being with the rest of her family and friends?

Wendy opened the box of chocolates from Marg and burst into tears. There, sitting on top of the chocolates, was a note.

Everyone who witnessed it was suddenly silent, but wait a minute – there was another box of chocolates from Purdys bought in Calgary. Would it have the same note, maybe some kind of a corporate quality check? It was carefully opened and there was no note. Just the one in the first box.

A heart-felt coincidence to be sure, but one that happened on this day, at this time, at this place, to this person and will never be forgotten.

When we got back to Edmonton, we went to Purdys, anxious to tell our wonderful story, especially to Betty. When we arrived, there were two ladies at the till. Neither was the one who had redecorated the box.

We asked when Betty would be working again so we could tell her the story, and the answer surprised us as one shook her head and the other said, "There's no one named Betty working here."

Whatever the origin of the first note, it became an instant keepsake, a special memory for this special day.

Believe it or not….

Still in the coincidence file, it was in December of 2020 that my Fitbit® started acting up. It wasn't charging properly. I didn't know if it was the watch or maybe the cube I was using to plug it into the power bar, or maybe the power bar itself. Whatever, it just wasn't charging.

This was a concern to me because I wanted to keep track of how many steps I was doing every day, especially at work. A couple of times a day I would go for a hike through the building, wearing my mask, across the top floor, down the stairs, hike to the back door and then around the kitchen. Sometimes, I would include a little trip around the parking lot.

I only walked. I never ran, because I did not want to be breathing heavily on my way back upstairs heading for the next newscast.

As Bryan Hall admonished in my book, *Welcome to Radio*, you must "never run to the microphone."

I liked to hit about four thousand steps a day, if possible. Now, I would never know for sure.

It was also during December that I was getting calls of congratulation and cards and emails and so forth about my forthcoming retirement at the end of the year. Someone asked if I would be getting a gold watch. I laughed. That may have been a corporate thing from decades before, not something that happens now; at least, not as far as I knew.

So, there I was, feeling not completely clothed at work, without my Fitbit®. Preparing the news, I was alternating between looking at the time in the corner of the computer screen and the clock on the wall. I found myself automatically pushing back my sleeve, only to be looking at a bare arm. On a hike downstairs, I depended on the clock in the kitchen to get me back upstairs on time.

Then the mail arrived, some letters and cards and a package from a fellow I had hired to work in the newsroom. His name was Tyler Loutan, and while I believed he had a great future in radio, he had decided to try something else in life, and I had wished him well as he left.

So, what was this package? I opened it up and found a six-sided box about four inches across. It was black and had a big gold "W" on the top. I wondered if that stood for Walmart.

I opened it up and was shocked at what I found. The W was explained inside the top of the box – Wittnauer.

And here's the part that may be hard to believe, it was *a gold watch*. And, with it, a beautifully written letter about his time with 630 CHED and GNR 880, and the mentors and friends he still had in the building.

I just sat there. I could never have seen this coming. Then I heard Marg's voice, hinting "Editorial, right?"

I started working on it right away. It would be my heart-felt, on-air note of appreciation.

Thank you, Tyler Loutan!

And now a Covid coincidence

I am writing this page on March 17, 2021, St. Patrick's Day. A couple of weeks ago, I arranged for my vaccination today. As I mentioned it in an email, I discovered that my brother Kirk, in Calgary, who has taught English in Siberia, Ecuador, and China, and in a growing number of countries, had also booked his shot for today. And my brother Ralph, who owns Your Dollar Store with More in Cardston, also had booked his vaccination for today. All on St. Patrick's Day. How does that happen?

As my wife, Marg, asked, "Were you all drinking the same Kool-Aid?"

If we were, it must have been green. Or, maybe it is just as Eileen Bell said, "You Laytons are just so darn competitive."

On stage

Chapter 16

Our trip to New York City was to cross off several things on our bucket list, including seeing a show on Broadway. We booked tickets in advance to see *Wicked* and enjoyed every minute. The theatre did not seem any better to me than the Northern Alberta Jubilee Auditorium; it was more the thrill of being on Broadway after years of hearing about it. We even experienced a buzz just standing in line waiting to get in.

We took a tour of the theatre district and then, following our son Chris's advice, we bought tickets to see a play called *Something Rotten*. It was a take-off on Shakespeare's *Hamlet* about some people putting on a play called *Omelet,* and it was hilarious.

Late that night, as we eased into our hotel room just off Times Square, we had to smile. The bed took up most of the room and we had to walk carefully around the edges. We are not big on spending a lot of money on hotels because we don't spend a lot of time in a room. We just want something safe and warm and dry because we are leaving early the next morning.

But now we were hungry. What to do? There was a pizza place across from the hotel, so I went down, crossed over the sidewalk that always seemed to have garbage on it, and made it through the traffic to the other side of the street.

As I looked over the selection of pizzas in the display case, I couldn't believe how big they were. I'd never seen such large pizzas. I told the fellow I wanted two small, personal size pizzas to go, please. I think that somehow, he guessed that I was a tourist.

"We don't have no small pizzas here – just what you see."

"But we don't want anything that big. Don't you make something smaller?" I asked.

"No," he explained, "you don't want a small pizza, you just want a *slice* of pizza."

I did not know they sold it by the slice, and I ordered two slices, expecting he would just throw a couple in a box and hand it to me. I was wrong. He put the slices in, arranged so they fit together without sticking together, along with some napkins. The slices were bigger than any other sliced pizza we had ever enjoyed, and we laughed as we held them by the crust with three fingers, bending it just a little, like we'd seen them do on the TV shows.

Next on our list would be to find the Apollo Theatre in Harlem where we had booked a tour. It was almost magical as the taxi dropped us off and we looked at the stars' names on the sidewalk: everyone from Ella Fitzgerald to James Brown. A couple of tour buses arrived and the front doors to the theatre were opened.

The tour guide was one of the best we had ever seen. He was an older man, who told us he had started at the theater as a boy, running errands for the stars, and told us many stories about them as we visited every corner of that building. We were just leaving the upstairs area, heading down into the seating area, when he said, "OK, we've still got 15 minutes left in this tour. Who would like to see a live performance on stage?"

The response was predictable, and he told us to hurry and get seats up at the front. Then he stood before us, and using his arm, he divided the front row into two groups. "This side," he said, "will sing a song. Someone sings the lead, the rest of you back-up or whatever you do best." There were some gasps of surprise, to which he responded, "Don't you tell me there's not a singer among you. Now get over to the other side – you've got five minutes to rehearse!"

Then, he gave the other group the choice of dancing or something else and a third group was also sent away to get ready.

Now, he came over to Marg and I, and pointing a finger, said, "And I want one of you on stage as well!"

I could hardly believe it – on stage at the Apollo?

Really?

Photo by Chris Layton

How I wished I had a puppet with me. Instead, I would do the opening to my comedy show that I had done probably hundreds of times before.

While the group ahead of me was performing – and they were good – the now emcee came over to me and said, "Tell me exactly how you want me to introduce you." I did.

When it came my turn, I walked onto the stage, and while I did the required good luck ritual the Apollo is known for, he was on the microphone, "And now, from Edmonton, Alberta, Canada, it's Baaaawb Lay-tuuuuun!"

I told my signature story about buying a jar of pickles (which I only ever do in public) and got a big laugh. As we were exiting the theatre, a lady came over and laughingly said, "That was a very funny story, Mr. Pickles!"

***   ***   ***

On many TV police shows staged in New York, they mention Hell's Kitchen. It sounds like a scary place. We asked and were told it was just a few blocks from our hotel. We had laundry to do and asked at the hotel if there would be a laundromat in Hell's Kitchen and were told there was. We found Hell's Kitchen and the laundromat and bought some food at a corner store while our clothes were being washed. There did not seem to be anything scary about the area, but we thought maybe bad things only happen at night, or just on TV shows.

On the way back, we came across a restaurant called Junior's. It had a sign out front claiming to have the best cheesecake in New York. Marg is a cheesecake fan, so we went in. She thought it was wonderful. To me, it just tastes like cake.

After our vacation we were watching *Blue Bloods* on TV, a police drama set in New York. It was near the end of the show and everyone was seated for Sunday dinner, but the youngest police officer, Jamie, had not yet arrived.

When he finally showed up, they asked why he was so late. He explained he had a last-minute call to Hell's Kitchen, but to make up for being late, he had brought everyone cheesecake from Junior's.

Marg and I looked at each other and said, gleefully, "Been there!"

In show business, it's called "product placement."

Another one off the bucket list...

We were both on stage at the Ryman Auditorium in Nashville. As we went on tour, the guide asked if we'd like a picture together on stage. As we got ready, he handed me a guitar because, he said, most people like to make it look like they are performing. I thought I would rather wait until I was really at the Grand Ole Opry, maybe wearing a Porter Wagoner outfit and singing a duet with Dolly Parton.

***   ***   ***

Not all experiences on stage are happy. I was tearing down equipment after a show and fell off the stage, injuring my left foot. Luckily, I could still drive home, but Sunday was agonizing, and Monday morning I had to really focus to get past the pain to read the news.

When I was done, I went to see Doctor Dominic Leung. He had been our family doctor for years and had our total trust. I limped into the examination room. After carefully looking at my foot, he informed me it was not broken. Doctor Leung told me I had two choices: I could either have him wrap it up and use crutches for a couple of weeks, or I could have acupuncture and likely walk out of there in a few minutes with no pain.

I had seen his acupuncture degree on the wall. I had also seen those acupuncture needles, and they did not look pleasant – they looked so awfully long. I thought about it for a moment, and could not imagine the needle hurting any worse than what I was already going through. I had come to trust him over the years and told him to go ahead and use a needle.

He told me to lie on my stomach and put my foot up in the air. I slowly bent my knee and did as I was told. I felt him use something to clean the area and then I said, "Wait – just before you stick it in, give me a warning so I can grab onto the edge of this table and get ready for the pain."

"Oh," he said, "it's already in."

I hadn't felt a thing. He asked if the foot pain was still there. It was. He flicked the top of the needle a couple of times with his finger and then adjusted the needle. I thought maybe he had pushed it in a tiny bit deeper.

"How it is now?" he asked.

I relaxed for a second to feel the effect. The pain was gone.

He told me to hop down onto the floor, but I was not hopping anywhere. I was not taking any chances with this new procedure. I gently put my foot down, starting with the toes, and slowly I put my weight onto my heel. There was no pain. I put on my socks and shoes.

I thanked him profusely and as we got to the registration desk, he informed me that Alberta Health did not cover acupuncture. Apparently, they were still deciding on covering it, although he was on a list of those approved to use it by the College of Physicians and Surgeons.

I did not care how much it cost, and I got out my wallet. He told me there would be no charge, but he wondered if there was a health care hearing on acupuncture, if I would be interested in speaking.

Just tell me the time and place.

That winter, I got my usual sinus pain and needed some medicine. As Doctor Leung looked me over, I jokingly asked if there was acupuncture for sinus problems. He said there was, indeed. Did I want to try it?

This one was a little scarier, because I could see the two long needles being pushed up on each side of the bottom of my nose, and there was a crunching sound. He told me that was normal. When he was finished, he told me to get home and grab a box of Kleenex, because my nose was going to start running like it never had before.

It did. And then it stopped, and I was fine.

And, after all these years, I have never had any more sinus pain.

Doctor Dominic Leung 1943-2017 Photo courtesy Leung family.

HOSPITALS
Chapter 17

It was while setting bowling pins in Al's Alley in Claresholm, Alberta, and sitting on the tiny shelf that divided two of the eight or ten alleys, that a pin flew up and hit me in the knee. I lost all feeling in that leg and they took me to the hospital. I was not in any pain; I just could not feel or use my leg.

I woke up in the middle of the night in that hospital bed. It was dark in the room except for a little flashlight, and as I looked, a doctor and a nurse were bending over me. The doctor was hitting around my knee with a little rubber hammer, trying to get a reflex. There was no response.

"Well," said the doctor to the nurse, "at least we know he's not faking it."

Another doctor came around the next morning, but the knee would not respond.

At noon we had some bland hospital food. Later they brought me some green Jell-O. As I ate the green Jell-O and wondered how much longer I would be in there, the feeling came back into my leg. I was able to move it back and forth. I climbed out of bed and stood on it. I walked around.

A nurse came in. "Where do you think you're going?"

"I think I'm going home!"

"I just came on shift," she said. "Looks like the doctor fixed your leg."

"No, the doctor couldn't make it work at all."

"So, what did?" She looked puzzled.

"It must have been the green Jell-O."

Opioids

In 2014, I needed a back operation. A nerve was being pinched that caused incredible pain in my left leg, and I needed crutches to walk. In that long wait for surgery, I was given Hydromorphone for the pain, an opioid.

It killed the pain but was also killing me on the air. My mouth was incredibly dry, and it felt like my lips and tongue were sticking together as I tried to read the news. No amount of water was helping.

Bryan Hall was the first to mention I did not sound right and asked if I was on something. This could not continue.

I had been assured I was not on enough of the drug to get addicted, but when the time came, I would need three weeks to slowly get off it, by cutting back a little at a time.

Upset that I was not sounding my best on the air, I decided to just quit over a weekend. I did not tell Marg what I was doing. How bad could it be?

The Friday night into Saturday was not too bad. During the day Saturday, I started to feel odd. Then, in the middle of the night on Saturday, I was awakened by my wife shouting at me and asking, "What is the matter with you?"

I was soaked in sweat, and she wanted to know why I was shaking so bad. She said the whole bed was vibrating. Thanks to her support, I made it through Sunday and dragged myself off to work Monday morning.

My doctor was shocked that I had done that, and luckily, the operation came soon after.

I do not pretend to know what someone addicted to opioids is going through. I'm sure in the grand scheme of things, mine was just a minor event.

While I now have empathy for those going through addictions and withdrawal, I feel we should have more resources on all sides of this issue, making a trafficker's future as tentative as his victim's.

Parking pain

I find myself from time to time in hospitals, visiting friends or family. I see many ranges of emotion as people pass by in the hallway.

Some are deep in thought. Others may be shedding silent tears of grief or relief.

I saw an elderly patient in the hallway in front of his room. They had taken him from his bed to sit in a chair for lunch. He kept trying to stand up but when he did, an alarm would sound. There was a little sign on the door to his room, warning that he had a "falling danger."

He was refusing to sit down and got angry as the staff tried to get him to sit down. I watched as they patiently coaxed him back into his chair and wondered if that would be me, some day.

One day, I was visiting Bruce Hammond. Some of you will remember him as radio DJ Jungle Jay from the Night-Time Zoo. Like his late mother, he was now stricken with Huntington's Chorea and was now spending his days in a bed or a wheelchair.

I had paid for my parking at the University Hospital in advance, but when I drove to the check-out ramp and inserted the ticket, the screen lit up with "Out of Order."

Now how would I get out? How would I get the barricade to raise?

Then I saw the problem. There was no barricade – it had been smashed to pieces – someone had crashed right through it.

I carefully drove over the pieces, wondering what torment the driver must have been in.

Snow Angels

Chapter 18

It was February 2nd, 2019, at about 8:30 in the morning. It felt like about -30 with the wind chill.

A man named José Marquez Lugo was on his way to Sunday morning services at the Church of Jesus Christ of Latter-Day Saints. The weather did not bother him. Heat, rain, wind, snow, or extreme cold, none of that mattered. Every week he was on the way to church – in his wheelchair.

José liked to get there early, so he could wheel around the parking lot and – using his picker-upper – collect any trash that might have blown in during the night. In the winter he would grab a snow shovel and use his battery-powered chair to push it along the sidewalk to make it safe for others.

He would get to church by taking the bus from his home to an intersection two blocks from the church on 142nd Street, and then use the big battery to push him the last two blocks.

On this day, after getting off the bus, he found the snow was too deep and he got stuck, unable to move. He rocked back and forth, like a car would, trying to get some traction, but he just got stuck even more.

He tried to use his cellphone to call for help, but something wasn't working. He was getting cold, and at that time on a

Sunday morning, there was no traffic and no pedestrians to ask for any help.

What could he do?

Well, he was, after all, on the way to church, so he offered a heartfelt, shivering plea for help from the Lord. Then, he sat there in the cold, waiting for an answer to his prayer.

There, with the cold pressing into his body, it must have felt like an eternity, but in fact, it was just a couple of minutes.

An ambulance was headed his way, being moved from one location to another, and the two paramedics operating it immediately sized up the problem. They stopped and tried to push him out of the deep snow, but the chair was stuck fast.

They knew they had to get him into the ambulance to keep him warm, but he and the chair with the big battery were too heavy to lift. They called their colleagues in the fire department. The response was swift, and the firefighters lifted him and his chair up into the warm ambulance.

He was checked out and found to be OK and very thankful. What more could they do for him?

They decided to drive him to church, just a couple of blocks away.

Imagine the looks on the faces of the other congregants arriving for church when an ambulance pulled into the parking lot, followed by a fire truck.

Firefighters lifted him down and before they left, the paramedics made sure he had a safe ride home.

Church members were always happy to help Hugo, but he valued his independence. At the time of this writing, waiting for the pandemic to end, he still plans to get to church in his wheelchair, and still gives thanks for his snow angels.

Paramedics Sarah Kennedy and Sheena Demkiew

Photos courtesy a grateful José Marquez Lugo.

Lessons to learn...
Chapter 19

Photo courtesy Kristin Raworth

It was late 2017, and movie mogul Harvey Weinstein was getting more personal publicity than he likely did for any of his company's movies. Allegations were coming in from actresses about sexual harassment and rape that stretched back more than 20 years.

The Weinstein Company board of directors fired the 65-year-old. He would reach settlements with some of the complainants but denied other allegations, including rape.

It would be months before he would be charged, and I believe in hearing both sides of a story before making a decision, and in having a constant conversation with my audience. I did an editorial asking if it was fair that he should be fired from his job without "due process." Suspended pending a trial I could understand, but to lose his job to allegations sounded like it might be a good topic for a debate.

Over the years, we had carried stories of sexual assault trials that ended in "not guilty" verdicts. Some had highlighted the issues of the victims not going to police until long after the alleged assault, and not even telling a friend about it. Others had the victims sending a nice email to the offender after the assault or even spending more time with him.

I had also been thinking of the "not guilty" verdict just the year before for Jian Ghomeshi, the former CBC Radio host. He was tried on four counts of sexual assault and one of choking. I recall the judge said something to the effect that just because the charges were not completely supported by the testimonies of the complainants, it was not the same as saying these things never happened.

It would be very seldom that any editorial I did on radio or television over 25 years would not get a flurry of comments. I would often use the best comments of the week to create my

"It's Fri-daaaay!" editorials. This one was no different. Most were from men, saying they had been falsely accused. One told me how he was experiencing a terrible divorce, and that his wife had suddenly accused him of some type of improper relationship with his children. He was denying it, but was not allowed to see his children. I would like to have heard his wife's side.

The most notable letter I received was from listener Kristin Raworth. She describes herself as an advocate for sexual violence survivors and suggested the examples I used from previous cases might be considered by some to be "victim blaming." That was not who I was. I just reported the facts as they came out in court. Still, she might have a point and I wanted to know more about what she was expressing.

I responded to her email and we eventually ended up on the phone discussing the topic. As we talked, I thought it would be a good idea to do a follow-up editorial to clarify the important points Kristin was making. For the first time in my career, I offered Kristin the opportunity to co-write the editorial to make sure I said it correctly.

As I write this now in April of 2021, Kristin recalls, in her own words:

"I have been advocating and speaking about sexual violence since 2016. In my experience, the most important part of that work is reaching out to folks and having discussions, including meeting them where they are and taking that as an opportunity to share. When I reached out to Bob, to be honest I didn't know if I would get a response. I can't say as I was the most gracious in my initial comments. I was extremely happy when he reached out, and even more so when he did so with a completely open mind about a topic that isn't easy for anyone, even professionals, to talk about sometimes.

"I am not just an advocate, but also a survivor of sexual violence, so the issue of victim blaming is a deeply personal one. When I came forward about my assault by a long-time friend, I was not believed or supported, and the people in my life found it easier to find fault in my behavior than in his. My experience is not unique; 80% of sexual assault survivors are assaulted by someone they know, meaning that when they disclose, they are often disclosing to someone who equally cares for their abuser. Victim blaming is one method people use to distance themselves from the survivor because then it is their fault, and not the fault of the abuser. This is why I felt it so vital to say something because with an audience there is responsibility and survivors are listening.

"I was grateful Bob worked with me on that editorial and on the common ground we came to writing it. He didn't have to do that, but he did, and it meant a lot to me, as I am sure it did to the folks who heard it. But what really meant a lot to me was the email Bob sent me when the editorial went up; he ended by telling me that my comments had changed his thinking on this issue.

"That touched my heart and is a testament to who Bob is, that not only was he willing to chat with me but that he was willing to examine his perspective on this issue and shift it. I treasure that email and the impact that editorial had."

For the rest of 2017 and into 2018, more horrible sexual assault allegations against Harvey Weinstein would come in, not just from actresses, but also from former employees. It seemed he wanted them to believe that the road to success began in his bedroom or his hotel, or wherever he deemed the "start line" to be. He has paid out many millions in settlements and is now serving 23 years in prison.

I wonder if they'll make a movie.

Reasons why...

With the Weinstein issue over, I welcomed more information so I could be better prepared to discuss such fragile issues as sexual assault, and the response of the victims that left so many of them vulnerable to good defense lawyers.

My continuing education would be closer than I thought. My daughter, Deborah Watson, has been a counsellor at a sexual assault centre for the past ten years, and has recently also started a private practice, Artful Mindful Playful, where she specializes in trauma as well as other diagnoses.

She explained to me that when people have been traumatized, they go into a survival response: they do what they think will bring them the most safety.

Especially when they will need to be near the person again (because the person who caused them trauma is a co-worker, part of their community such as a church member or neighbor, or particularly a boss), they might become submissive (a "fold" response), or "fawn," which is when they try hard to tend and befriend the person in the hope they will not be harmed again. This might look like friendly emails the next day (sound familiar?) or otherwise acting like nothing happened. They may be too ashamed or devastated to reach out to others – they may blame themselves for not fighting or running away, not recognizing they used a different survival response because it is not a conscious decision – it is an automatic response learned much earlier in life through their particular circumstances. The fear of being rejected by people if they found out might be too great to allow reaching out, because to be abandoned would be unbearable.

In other words, response to sexual assault might look odd to someone who has either not had to go into a survival response when faced with threat and danger because they have power (think police officers and judges), or whose survival response was different.

I'm starting to understand.

Thank you, Debi. Guess you did some homework after all.

Words

It was in the late 1970s and women's activism was growing. I had no problem with their demands. After all, I had a mother and sisters and a wife and a daughter, and I wanted every opportunity for them.

I had just done a story on how, after a heavy rain, a manhole cover had blown off. I got a call telling me it was not proper to call it a manhole cover. This was a new one on me. The caller was explaining that if women could get the proper training, they could also work in the underground systems, and it was just not fair how they were denied these opportunities.

I asked what I should call them instead.

The reply? "Drain access points" would work.

Then there was the time I announced that a local ski hill was opening with "man-made snow." The phone rang shortly thereafter, and I was informed that the term "man-made snow" was demeaning to women. It suggested that women were not capable of making it.

It was another new one on me, and I asked for a better way of describing it that would be acceptable to all.

The answer was, "artificial snow."

It would be some time after this conversation that the next leg of this story would appear. I was in a hotel for a meeting, and as I entered the front door there was a line-up ahead of me, beside some wooden barricades. There was a hole in the center of the lobby with a pile of dirt and muck, and what looked like a piece of rusty, broken pipe.

It was quite a way from us, but the hotel was keeping people close to the wall and we worked our way around to the meeting room. As I got further along, I could see the sign that proclaimed: Caution – Men Working.

I knew better than that.

As a hotel staffer came along the line to greet us and assure us that everything was okay and the water service had been restored, I pointed to the sign, and told him some of his guests may be offended by it.

He wondered what I was talking about, and as I proceeded to give him a lesson, a woman just a couple of people behind me spoke up with, "I don't know who you think you are, but shut the hell up!"

I turned to her, "But..." I started.

"But nothing, just move along!"

"The sign says men working, and I was just explaining that..."

"I know where you are going, and I've heard it all."

"But – *men* working?"

"The sign is correct," she said. "If women were doing this job, there would not be all this mess!"

Lesson learned. If it was today, we'd talk about me being "woke," but back then I just learned to keep my mouth shut.

A true radio legend...
Chapter 20

Bruce Bowie

Just one of the great people I worked with in my career was popular 630 CHED morning show host, Bruce Bowie. It was truly a sad day for me when he announced his retirement. I had come to know him not only as a consummate broadcaster, but as a truly kind human being.

Wanting to preserve his memory, I asked him several questions. Here are the answers in his own words.

Question 1: What were the greatest things you experienced in your career?

Bruce: "I saw many great things happen in my career, most due to our great listeners. While working mornings for CISN, for three different years I lived on the street to raise money for Hope Mission. It was a three-day stint that always ended with a radiothon the final day.

"On year two, we were very pleased when over $60,000 was raised. By year three, management trusted me enough to say, 'You pick the goal this year.' So, after a great deal of thought and prayer, on my second day out, while Chris Scheetz interviewed me from back at the station, I announced a goal of $125,000.

"There was a lot of silence on the other end.

"A few moments after I hung up, my phone rang with them asking me, basically, if I was a bit crazy. This was a lot of money to ask. With all the other fund-raising efforts we have, this was asking too much. They didn't want us to sound like we were always begging. In fact, to further that plan, the radiothon the next day, rather than going until 5:00 in the afternoon, would end after my show at 9:00 in the morning.

"So, here I was with twice the goal and a fraction of the time to raise it. I should not have doubted. It didn't happen at 9:00, but by the time the news finished at 9:05, a final call came in that pushed us over $125,000. More came in after that throughout the day, and I will be forever grateful."

Question 2: What touched your heart?

Bruce: "There are many things that have touched my heart. I thought I was pretty solid and would be able to handle the Stollery Children's Hospital Radiothons. I had gotten used to the fact that at least once there would be a story of what a child or family had gone through that would lead to tears.

"Perhaps the most difficult day for me was the morning we were on air and the call came into the newsroom that Jerry Forbes had died. I guess I didn't realize how much he meant to me and how much of a father figure he had become. It is the only time that I became flat-out messed up, almost unable to talk while crying on air.

"My program director called, concerned that I might not be able to carry on. Somehow, we soldiered through. I know that for countless thousands of kids who had toys from 630 CHED Santas Anonymous, Jerry continues to be a father figure to this day."

Jerry Forbes 1923-1981   Photo courtesy Marty Forbes

Question 3: What changes have you seen in radio?

Bruce: "The main changes I have seen over 47 years is in just how things are done. Of course, at the start, there was no social media but there is a lot of emphasis on that now. It is much easier to text, but I miss talking to people on the phone. And, as with many businesses, more is being expected with fewer people. I used to love all the characters that were part of the morning show. So many people bouncing things off one another lead to some real magic and fun on the air."

Question 4: How did you manage to stay so kind to some of those people?

Bruce: "I have tried to learn from the best. Bob Layton always told me that if someone on the phone called you an idiot, rather than getting into it with them, it's best just to agree and move on. I can't say I have always been good at following that advice, but it is good advice. The good news is that those callers are few and far between. Most are truly kind, forgiving, and supportive. I have made many friends over the years with relationships that started through a radio speaker."

Question 5: What advice do you have for new broadcasters?

Bruce: "When I started, a wise veteran of the business advised I pour myself into the job and learn as much as I could and soak it all in early. Don't turn down emcee opportunities. He said it was best to do all this early, because once I was married and even after that with children, I needed to give them more time than my career, so get established, first. That is good advice. Also, at some point in a new broadcaster's career, they may be asking themselves, 'What am I even doing here – couldn't I be making more money selling shoes at the mall?' Those who think that are probably in the wrong business. There *has* to be an insatiable desire for broadcasting."

Question 6: Have you any regrets?

Bruce: "Yes, I do. I didn't always follow the advice and there were too many times my family made the sacrifice while dad was off working somewhere. As well, I should not have been so nervous early on. Every time the boss's door was closed, I was sure it was plans for my firing. By God's grace, in an industry where most get fired or laid off at least once, if not several times, it never happened.

"I spent too much time in worry over things that were not an issue. I should have spent more time just soaking it in, enjoying it all and trying to realize how we were all blessed. In those early days of 630 CHED, we owned the airwaves and didn't realize what we had.

"Marty Forbes recently reminded me of the Bicycle Picnics we would have at Hawrelak Park, where we invited people to cycle down for a free concert. It got too big for Hawrelak, so we moved and heavily promoted the new Rundle Park location. As that large park filled and jammed with people that went all the way up the hill and back to the golf course, it became a matter of concern for the city.

"They made a number of demands for the next year that made it economically unfeasible, and that wound up being the last year. That experience taught me about the power of radio. There is a lot I will miss, like the chance to put a show together and be creative, but mostly I will greatly miss the people, both inside the station and the listeners at the other end."

(End of Interview)

Bruce, as for you missing the people, after a large number of phone calls, I can truly tell you the feeling is mutual.

And yes, Jerry Forbes left a great legacy in our community. Not just the many broadcasters who flourished under his guidance, but his effect on the many thousands of children blessed by 630 CHED Santas Anonymous. The Jerry Forbes Centre for Community Spirit is such a fitting tribute.

Let me share something with you that will demonstrate how he saw things.

It was in 2014 that a listener, Eleanor Halarneau (apologies if I'm not reading the writing correctly), sent me a letter. She told me how she had been at a garage sale and picked up a box of what was supposed to be scrap paper for her children to colour on.

Among the many sheets of paper, she found four writings entitled "Thought for Today," written by Jerry Forbes for use on-air in July of 1964. She wrote that since they had been around for 50 years, and were so beautifully written, she thought someone who knew Jerry might like to have them.

She especially liked the one for Monday, July 6, 1964.

Here's what Jerry wrote:

"There are many great lessons on life to be learned from the world around us. Last summer, while travelling through the swamps and everglades of the Florida peninsula, I was impressed by the fact that from out of the muck and mire of the teeming swamp came the most breath-taking trees and flowers.

"There they were, rooted in the steaming filth of the semi-tropical jungle, yet reaching up to the heavens, gloriously beautiful, refusing to bend back down to the darkness that had given them birth.

"Sometimes, in life, we meet people like that. People who have had none of the advantages of life, people who were born into unhappy homes, and surrounded by misery and evil throughout their formative years. And yet, like the flowers of the jungles and the swamps, they refused to bend down to the mire from whence they came, and instead fought their way up through the darkness to the sunshine above.

"I admire such people so very much. They must surely have greatness of heart. They must certainly have incredible courage and a deep and abiding love for beauty.

"Above all, they have self-respect, without which they would most assuredly sink back to the gloom that surrounded them at birth.

"I have known such people, and they have enriched my life beyond all measure. They give courage and faith. They give dedication and beauty. They underline the fact that truly there are extraordinary possibilities in the ordinary person."

- Jerry Forbes

Grandpa's gift...
Chapter 21

As each of my grandchildren reached the age of 14, I had a new tradition waiting for them. I would take those who were available to the Edmonton Flying Club and let them fly a plane. It was called a Discovery Flight, with the student and the instructor up front, and me in the back with my camera.

I wanted them to experience something totally different, and as a past member of the Calgary Flying Club, I knew how exciting this could be. Each one loved it.

I tweeted out that I was about to take my granddaughter Cadence up for a flight. She was thrilled because she would finally have bragging rights like her older brother, Javan, who had been up a couple of years before.

I got a call from newspaper columnist Cam Tait. He wanted to know about this tradition, and when I explained what it was like for them, he asked if he could interview them for an article.

I said I would see how they felt about it, and they were in favor, so a date was set.

Cadence and Javan live outside of Edmonton, so it was a nice drive to get them into the city and drive to Cam's place. I was glad for the long drive because there was something I needed to tell them about this interview.

Having talked with Cam many times over the years (see my book *Welcome to Radio*) on the phone, I had developed enough respect for him to listen carefully as he spoke. His life has not been easy. He did not breathe when he was first born and developed Cerebral Palsy. He uses a wheelchair. His speech can be difficult for some to understand at times, but his journalistic intelligence shines through.

As we drove along, I explained all of this to my two grandchildren. I told them that despite what some see as handicaps, Cam went to school and became a successful columnist. He has written about major events, and now, he's going to write about you.

I told them that along with being very bright teenagers, today they would be treated as adults, being asked questions about their lives, and that they needed to respond as adults by listening closely to what Cam would ask.

I also gave them a course in how to be interviewed as adults, which meant the answer to a question like, "What was it like to fly a plane?" is not "good, fun, fine," or some other one-word answer. They needed to reply with a complete sentence, being as descriptive as they could, touching on anything from the physical feeling to emotions. I told them not to be afraid to talk too much, because the final result would be edited for space and Cam would want lots to select from.

We arrived at Cam's place and sat across the table from him. What happened next was a surprise to me.

Cadence, Cam, and Javan.

After introductions were done, Cam, in the biggest voice I have ever heard him use, looked at the pair and said, "IF YOU DON'T UNDERSTAND WHAT I AM ASKING – SAY SO! I'M USED TO THAT. JUST TELL ME AND I'LL SAY IT AGAIN. OK?"

Then in a softer tone, he began asking his questions. They were thoughtful. They were well prepared. They were deep. They were fun.

Cam did not have a list of questions before him on paper. He was listening to answers and forming the next questions. I knew Cam was a pro, but I had never seen him do an interview before.

I was impressed.

It would be a learning lesson for me as well as my grandchildren. The resulting newspaper article will be a keepsake, forever.

PS: Javan, who plays several musical instruments, got himself a job giving lessons at a music store. It felt good to hear the boss told him he really "aced the interview."

Ducks on the lake...
Chapter 22

I had a call from Canadian Forces Base Cold Lake, Alberta. They were hosting Exercise Maple Flag, a gathering of Canadian and international fighter pilots and crews for air combat training and they wanted me to speak. They told me that after a hard day of flying, they could use some humour.

They asked what my speaking fee would be, and after thinking about that, I decided that instead of the long drive up there, I would rather fly in one of those planes. The response I received was that although their planes were regularly at Canadian Forces Base Namao, near where I lived in Edmonton, it was not within protocol to send a plane for me. They said they'd be happy to give me a ride there and back, but it would have to be on whatever aircraft was heading for Cold Lake that day.

I agreed.

The day of the talk arrived, and I drove out to Namao, wondering what kind of fighter jet I would be in, and whether it would take more than just a few very exciting minutes to make the trip, and what it might be like to wear an oxygen mask. I arrived at Namao and met the pilot and two others flying with him. So, there would be four in the plane. Hmmm. I wondered how that would work.

Now we were walking towards a helicopter, and the pilot explained that this would be a longer flight to get to Cold Lake than usual, because this crew was being trained in search and rescue. They had made some notes on the way down on what they observed in various farms and fields, and today they'd be seeing if they could notice any change, among other things.

Not quite what I had expected, but it should still be very interesting.

It turned out to be much more interesting than I had imagined.

One of the crew was sitting up front with the pilot. The other was sitting in the back with me.

As we lifted off, one of the crew said, "Power lines to the left."

The plot responded, "Roger that, power lines to the left."

Seemed odd. I had noticed the power lines and I was sure the pilot must have.

Then it was, "Crossing a main highway." The pilot responded to the affirmative.

As we crossed over a farm, there was some discussion about what was different from yesterday. There was talk about how the tractor that was near the barn yesterday was now sitting down by the main gate, and some other things.

In the distance I could see a lake coming, and sure enough, one of the crew said, "Lake coming." The pilot confirmed the observation.

I could see there were ducks on the lake, and the fellow next to me said, "Ducks on the lake!" with a little more urgency than the other comments.

The pilot confirmed what I was sure he must have already seen that there were, indeed, ducks on the lake.

A moment later, one of the crew said, "Ducks are still on the lake."

This was getting a little weird. Did these guys have no lives? I wondered.

The pilot, looking down at the lake, confirmed the ducks were still on the lake.

And there came another observation and confirmation that the ducks had not lifted off.

There were other things they talked about regarding the landscape and changes in other things from yesterday's training flight.

As we got close to Cold Lake and the air base, I could see other planes in the sky.

As a former member of the Calgary Flying Club, I had been in this situation flying in and out of the Calgary International Airport and I was scanning our flight path, when one of the crew members said, "Traffic at eleven o'clock." I had seen that, and I was sure the pilot must have, but he responded to confirm it. The same with the traffic at four o'clock that I had already seen.

I guessed this must be how they do things in the military, but to my young mind at the time, it seemed a little overdone, sort of like everyone was stating the obvious. I was waiting for someone to say, "Today is Friday," so that the date could also be confirmed. Perhaps this was part of their training, to see how observant everyone was. I knew there had to be a reason, and I was anxious to find out what it was.

Eventually, we landed, and as I climbed out, the pilot asked me if I had any questions. I was a guest, so I had to be polite and tactful, but I was still a newsman with questions. I asked why the crew pointed out everything from power lines to ducks on the lake and even that they were… uh… still on the lake.

The pilot smiled as though he had heard this question before and said, "Come with me." We entered a building and went down a hallway to place where a lot of pictures were hung on a wall. I looked closely. They were pictures of crashed aircraft.

The pilot explained that this is what can happen if you assume the pilot has seen what you are looking at. He said, in effect, "Maybe the pilot is having a bad day and not really focusing. Maybe he's got trouble at home on his mind. Maybe he's been drinking…" Although, he was quick to point out a pilot is not supposed to drink before he flies.

I nodded, thinking of the stories I had done in the news about a couple of instances where pilots of passenger planes who had been drinking had been pulled out of the cockpit after a complaint from a co-pilot or flight attendant.

The pilot continued, "Safety has to come first, and we fly as a team, each looking out for the other." I felt silly about what I had thought in the air, and then he continued, "About the ducks on the lake. If they had lifted off, it could have been a bit of a shock to you. I would have done a hard turn and powered up to get out of the way. That picture over there shows what ducks can do to you if you are not paying attention." Now I really felt ignorant.

The car had arrived that was to take me over to the hall where I would be speaking after a supper. The driver and a passenger were in the front. I was on the back seat.

We came to a runway and the car stopped. The driver got out and knelt beside the car. I jokingly said to the passenger, "What... is he... praying?"

The passenger laughed and explained he was checking the tires to see if there were any little rocks or chunks of mud or anything. "You see that bucket on the pole over there?" he said.

I looked. There was a red bucket on a pole with white letters F O H.

"Anything we don't want left on the runway," he explained, "goes in that bucket."

"F O H?" I asked.

"Foreign object hazard."

The bucket used at Bob's safety seminars.

We drove across the runway and stopped again. The driver got out of the car and walked back to the runway, squatting down to have a look at it.

When he got back into the car, I asked if he minded me asking what exactly he was doing.

He explained that he was checking to see if anything, even a little bit of dirt, had fallen from the underside of the car.

"When a fighter is doing a touch and go," he said, "and they go full throttle to take off again, that powerful jet engine could suck up anything on the runway. Even a pebble from my car tire could possibly lead to engine failure and maybe even a plane falling out of the sky."

When I returned home, I designed a PowerPoint safety seminar entitled Ducks on the Lake. As each person enters the meeting, I give them a little, highly polished pebble to put in their pocket. When the seminar is over, I tell them if they don't want the pebble they can drop it in the bucket, or they can take it to work and put it on their desk beside their pen holder as a daily safety reminder.

I would always hear some pings in the bucket as people left, but there were not as many pebbles as I gave out.

As I write this, in 2021, I wonder how much safer our streets would be if cars were handled the same way as helicopters, although, I must admit, hearing your passenger tell you the traffic light has turned red and a car is coming up to pass you on the right and you confirming it, may get a little irritating for some.

Bottom line for me, my wife, Marg, is a more valuable co-pilot than I had ever realized.

Intercourse

Chapter 23

My wife Marg is a quilter. She had read a lot about Amish quilting, and there we were, planning to visit Amish country in Pennsylvania.

It was great fun at work, as the people in the 630 CHED/GNR 880 newsroom asked each other what they were planning to do for the summer vacation. One said, "I'm doing Disneyland." Another said, "I'm doing Las Vegas." As eyes fell on me, the little devil on my shoulder wanted me to say, "I'm doing intercourse," but there were strict rules at Corus about saying anything someone might find suggestive, so I explained that we were going to Pennsylvania to see Amish country. One of their main communities is called Intercourse, which has to do with communication, not what usually jumps to most minds.

However, as I would later learn, there was also an intimate aspect to the area.

We joined a tour that took us to quilting displays and the tour bus drove very carefully down the highways to their farms, giving proper space to the Amish horse drawn carriages.

We went to a one-room Amish schoolhouse and had a picture taken holding hands; a picture that would lead to a national award-winning editorial called "Life School."

We drove from farm to farm, seeing how they ran successful operations without being "on the grid" for utilities, although one farmer did admit to us that he had a telephone in the barn. It was for business or emergencies though, not just for talking or wasting time.

Back on the road to the next farm I thought I saw something that made me take a second look. In a shelter beside a building, I thought I saw a camel. Yes, a camel. I took a second look as the bus made a turn, and sure enough – it was a camel.

I went to the front of the bus and spoke with the tour guide and he told me that was our next stop.

The farmer had a couple of camels and explained how they fed them and so on. People were surprised, but no one was asking many questions, so I put on my newsman's hat and asked, "Why are you raising camels?"

He told us that camel milk sells for $125.00 a gallon.

The group, mostly seniors, looked at me as I asked, "Really? Who pays that much money for camel milk?"

He answered, "Some Middle Eastern men. They believe it gives them more… uh…" and he made an outward motion with his hand just below his belt buckle that was sort of an open-handed, repeated, waving. I wondered if the Amish had a word for "aphrodisiac."

The cautious laughter showed there was likely no one in the crowd who did not understand the meaning of the sign language he was using.

When we got back home, I told 630 CHED's morning man, Bruce Bowie, on the air about the camel milk and how much it sold for. We jokingly discussed buying a camel and starting our own business in Edmonton.

A listener would suggest there was some fermentation involved in giving camel milk this unique quality.

Later, in 2018, CNN ran a piece on camel milk that explained how a different protein composition made it closer to human milk than cow's milk, and therefore, less allergenic. The article also mentioned some evidence was emerging that camel's milk may also help to control diabetes and some symptoms of autism.

As I would learn, many times over, travel can be so educational.

And... rewarding... as this photo by Rob Hislop shows.

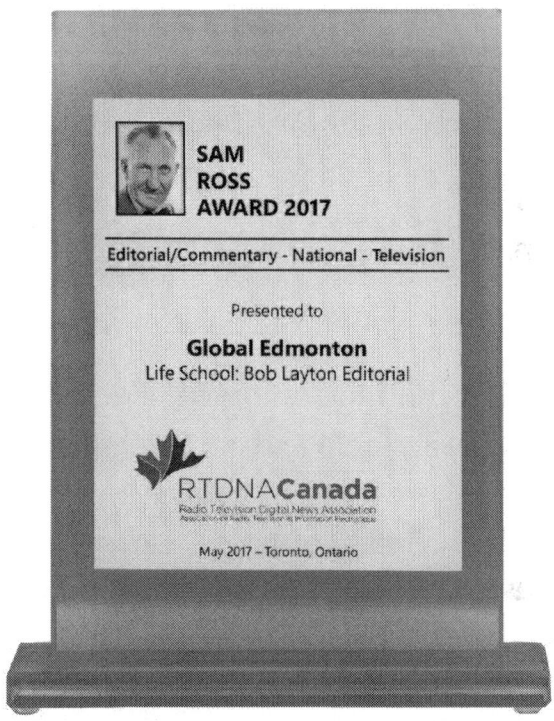

Back in the saddle, again...

More surprises would come as we headed for Branson, Missouri. The hills were so many it was like a roller coaster ride, and to make it even more interesting, it was raining heavily.

I had never driven in such a rainstorm for that long. It lasted all day. It was getting dark, so we decided to find a motel in the next town, which turned out to be Buffalo. We found a motel quickly, and it offered breakfast as well.

Shortly after we arrived, the storm got worse. We could hear it pounding on the walls of our room, which was down a small flight of stairs. We went to sleep to the rhythm of the rain.

We wanted to get an early start the next morning, so we arose early, about the time breakfast would be ready. Problem: we had no electricity. The lights would not come on. The bathroom was, of course, totally dark. I thought I'd check with the office and when I opened the door, the hallway was also dark.

Looking in the direction of the office, I saw the stairs we had come down, lit with a candle and glow-sticks on each step. The manager was also there, explaining that the storm had knocked out the power to their side of town. He apologized that there would be no breakfast. He said the power was still on a block away, and that there was a McDonalds there where we could eat.

We had hoped to try something more local in each place but wanted to get on the highway, so we stopped at McDonald's and went inside. While the food was not Missouri-specific, the atmosphere was.   The walls were decorated with a western theme, and there was a section where instead of seats, they had saddles!

Saddles in the McDonald's at Buffalo, Missouri

Time, Or Money

Chapter 24

We learned long ago that everything costs either time or money. Instead of buying something, you could make it yourself. It would take more of your time, but it would cost a lot less.

That was the same reasoning we used to drive to Branson, Missouri. The plane fare was more than we wanted to pay, and I do not enjoy sitting around for hours at airports. I do enjoy sitting and listening to country music, and they have dozens of shows a day in Branson.

Driving would take a few days, but the cost of food and lodging and gasoline was a lot less than two plane tickets.

As we got close to Branson, there was a building just off the highway that advertised show tickets, and we pulled in. I had expected to just see a ticket wicket, but that was not the case. A lady took us to a table to sit down and see all the show ads. As we chose what we wanted to see, based on the entertainers, I was looking at the prices, and the lady told us we could see all the shows for free and get a hotel at a reduced rate as well, if we just attended a one-hour meeting where they would tell us about other vacations that were available.

A one-hour meeting in return for free shows sounded like spending time instead of money, and that might be okay, but it sounded a lot like a Time Share meeting we were invited to once in Hawaii, where when we arrived, they wanted my credit card number "in case" we decided to buy something.

Since we were at the Branson ticket stop in the morning, and I was hesitant about signing up for this, the lady made a call and arranged for a hotel room for us at no charge, so we could relax and get unpacked before the meeting in the afternoon.

We signed up.

The hotel was nice, with an advertised free breakfast menu better than anything we had seen on our motel trip so far.

Then came the meeting. They did not ask for our credit card in advance – no, they wanted more than that: our passports!

"Passports?" I asked, perhaps sounding a little incredulous. "Passports? What do you want with our passports?"

"We just want to take a scan for our records."

"Why?"

"Because you're from out of the country, and that is our company's policy."

I wanted a fuller explanation, but they offered none, and I declined to hand over my passport. They told me we would not be admitted to the session, and we were escorted out of the room to a booth to have our name removed from the show ticket list. There were people sitting nearby, waiting to be taken into the main room.

As we approached the booth, the young lady there smiled and said, "I hope you're having a wonderful day!"

I replied, "I would, except I feel discriminated against by your company, and I don't understand why."

She got a puzzled look on her face, and I noticed other people sitting nearby turning to look.

"We're from Canada, and they won't let us in without a passport. It's like we look like criminals, or something."

Now the people sitting nearby were looking interested, and the man escorting us out had noticed the discussion was generating some attention from others waiting to be welcomed in.

He did the right thing.

He took us away from there, over to a side wall where no one could hear us, and said, "Look, this is just company policy. I'm not even sure why, but here's what I'll do. Your show tickets are being cancelled, but you are already in the hotel, so we can let you stay there."

Sounded good to me, and we left.

We headed over to the buffet at the Golden Corral. On the way out, there was man in a kiosk surrounded by show posters. He asked how long we were in town for, and we told him we had just arrived. He asked what shows we wanted to see, and I thought he was selling tickets, so we came in close to look at the posters.

Guess what happened next.

He told us to pick three shows to see for free if we would just attend a one-hour presentation on other vacation opportunities. I told him we had just been there but had been denied because I wouldn't hand over my passport.

He told us his company did not ask for passports.

"How about a credit card?" I asked. "Will they want one in advance?"

"No, nothing like that. Just listen to a one-hour presentation, that's all. If you decide not to join, you just take your show tickets and leave."

Free show tickets sounded good, but we did not want to add any more stress to what was supposed to be a vacation, full of the country music that I love. Marg and I looked at each other for a moment. We did get a free hotel out of the first one, so if an hour's time can get us more than a hundred-dollars-worth of tickets, what have we got to lose?

We agreed to try it and he asked if we wanted center or aisle seats for the shows. He told us he would make the arrangements, and we would receive our tickets after the presentation.

For some reason, in my mind, I saw the presentation as being in a kind of hall with a presenter, and maybe a video up front. Not quite. It was a hall, but full of round tables with large balloons attached to each one, floating just overhead.

A salesman took us to a table and began his pitch with the expected questions to get to know us, and about who we were and where we were from, and where we liked to vacation.

He told us a sad story about the passing of his father some time ago. It did not seem to fit the narrative and I was not sure what the effect was supposed to be. Sympathy, maybe?

Then, we were asked to make a list of vacation spots we would like to visit, so that he could show us they were available. Then more about his dad. Hmmm.

He took us on a drive to see a beautiful home that we would be able to use from time to time. We really liked the bright blue kitchen cupboards. I explained to him that in Edmonton, there was a lawyer who advertised he would get you out of a Time Share agreement, and I asked if there was a down-side to this deal. He said he had never heard of lawyers doing such a thing in Branson and explained to me that this was not a "Time Share," it was a "Fraction Share," something he said was totally different.

He took us back to the hall and as we entered, there was a loud POP. Someone had just used a pin on a balloon and people were applauding. He explained that the celebration meant someone had just signed up.

As he began his closing, asking questions designed for positive answers, we heard two more pops, but also saw other tables where people were leaving, and the balloons were untouched.

He asked if we liked the idea for vacations that he had shown us, and we agreed that we did. He suggested a price to us that was way above our budget, and when we turned that down, he had a different offer at a much lower price.

As I waited to see what might come next, he asked if I had any concerns he could address. I explained to him that while he might be an expert in helping people buy into Fraction Shares, I really knew nothing about it and wanted to be careful.

He agreed that was a good idea and offered to explain more about it.

I told him that before I made a final decision that might well be "yes," I wanted a copy of the contract to send to my accountant and lawyer for their approval.

If everything was as he told me, I was sure they would approve it and we would break the balloon. "What do you say?"

He said, "No." They didn't really have time for that. The shares were in demand.

I told him that using a fax would only take a few minutes and it might be well worth his while. He was starting to look very uneasy.

He began to take us in a different direction, and Marg pointed out that we were told this would only take an hour, and it had already been an hour and a half. He replied that what they meant was an hour for each of us, followed by a kind of forced laugh.

He seemed a little frustrated and asked us to come to a different table, over in the corner. We walked around the people who were leaving with their balloons still floating and sat at a much smaller table. He gave a little wave and another man joined us. He had an even better offer, one that came with a low price but would still get you into the program. He asked how we could possibly turn that down.

I told him it was the best offer I'd heard all day, and it sounded great!

He smiled at the other guy, who looked very relieved.

Then I asked for a copy of the contract to be approved by my people back home. He said they did not have time to do that, and told us we were making a mistake in turning them down.

I pointed out that it was *them* who turned *us* down.

"Just give them the tickets," said the final closer to the salesman as he got up and left.

We were about the last people leaving the balloon room as we were again escorted to a booth, only this time we collected our show tickets, and those aisle seats were great.

The next day, driving to a show, was when I saw the sign. It was a legal firm advertising that they could get you out of a Time Share.

The sign said nothing about a Fraction Share.

How could it?

Fraction Shares are totally different.

Um, they are, aren't they?

But wait – there's more!

Branson had been a wonderful experience, all things considered. We had stayed in that great hotel with the delicious breakfast and attended many great shows, many at no charge.

You could do a breakfast show with live music, a lunch show, a mid-afternoon performance, a supper show, an evening show and even a late-night gospel show! I got my much-needed country and western and bluegrass music fix. The prices were reasonable, and the food was just what we wanted. We visited many places from the Golden Corral to Starvin' Marvin's.

And a side note: We discovered Missouri makes the best cornbread we had ever tasted.

We headed for South Dakota, with no idea what we were about to discover. We could see it in the distance on a bluff above the Missouri River. As we got closer, we could see a statue of some kind, and luckily it was part of a rest stop at a place called Chamberlain.

What a sight! It was a fifty-foot steel statue of an Indigenous woman holding a star quilt. The metal diamond shapes on the quilt, more than a hundred of them in a striking blue colour, moved – as the tourism info said – like leaves in the breeze.

At the information center we would learn it was designed to honour the cultures of the Lakota and Dakota people. It had been gifted to the state in honour of the 125th anniversary of South Dakota.

Its purpose is to show that the state's native cultures are very much alive and standing with dignity.

Appropriately, the name of the statue is Dignity.

Photo Courtesy Travel South Dakota

We were awe-struck by its beauty and the message it gave so clearly.

As I update this book, it is June 21, 2021. It is National Indigenous Peoples Day. My mind goes back to my first job in radio in 1970 at CKNL in Ft. St. John, B.C.

Many people in the outer part of our listening area had no telephones, and part of our job in the community was to relay personal messages that everyone could hear.

I had to go on-the-air and tell the Indigenous community that a baby had died, along with a message from the mother on how it could possibly have been saved, if one of the cars on the highway had just stopped and given her a ride to the doctor.

I was so upset over how it happened, I discussed leaving radio with my boss and mentor, Mel Stevenson.

This tragic story is in my book, *Welcome to Radio*, also on Amazon.

Rwanda Rob

Chapter 25

When I was News Director at 630 CHED, Rob Hislop came to work for me twice – in 2002 and again in 2010.

The first time was after a stint at CTV for ten years.

The second time was after doing the morning show and supper news at Citytv.

He was very good on the air, and among the many talents Rob has is photography.

He would leave CHED in 2012 to further his career, photographing everything from weddings to products to national and international sporting events.

I would call on Rob to do my first photos with my puppets.

I would need him again when I planned this book, because I wanted photos of some of my awards. I found it impossible to get a proper picture, because they all had a shiny surface and I kept getting reflections of overhead lighting, and if I got closer, me.

Rob knew exactly what to do, as you will see later in this book.

And not only that – he designed this book's terrific cover!

But what he did for me pales in comparison to what he did in Rwanda.

There he ended up face to face with a mountain gorilla. Not just any mountain gorilla, but the dominant male silverback. Fortunately, he had a camera in each hand for protection.

Let's let Rob tell how that happened, in his own words:

"It took me a long time to get to Africa, as it had been a dream of mine since my University of Alberta days. So, let's just round it off to about 40 years.

"As luck would have it, my ability to talk – a lot – helped with the process. I was having coffee with a friend of mine, Marion. I was telling her about my Africa dream and said maybe it's time to give up on it, and if it didn't happen I was okay with it. The next thing I knew, Marion, through a cousin, managed to connect me with the director of an NGO out of Calgary. The next thing I knew I was getting the required shots and packing my bags for rural Ethiopia and a two week stay with the group HOPEthiopia.

"I stayed at the group's location in Harbu Chulule. An orphanage was on the site, and as a result my cameras got a lot of work over my stay, both by myself and any of the two dozen children living there who managed to snag one."

Photo courtesy Rob Hislop

"The main part this trip was a dental mission, and I was the photographer. A handful of locations were chosen for the free dental care provided by four Alberta-based dental professionals.

"The process was simple. A patient walks in. Gets some freezing. And out comes a tooth. My job was to take pictures of the procedure. Also helping out was a cataract surgeon from Addis Ababa. That gave me an opportunity to photograph cataract surgery in a room that was lined with plastic and duct tape to cover the holes in the wall. It was fascinating and amazing to see people walk in blind, and leave knowing they would soon be able to see.

"My first encounter with Africa (Ethiopia) was everything I could have hoped for and I wanted to go back. So, I did. It turns out HOPEthiopia also operates in Rwanda.

"After thinking I would never make it to Africa, I ended up going there twice in ten months. This time we stayed in Kigali, an urban setting which was much different from rural Ethiopia. Like that trip, this one was highlighted by meeting such amazing people.

"That's what made the main reason why I wanted to see Rwanda that much more difficult. The 1994 Genocide in the small African country had always puzzled and intrigued me. I went to a number of memorial sites, and to say those visits were emotional is an understatement.

"The country has recovered a lot over the following years. One of the sectors spurring on growth is tourism. A main attraction is the Mountain Gorilla. With only 1000 left in the wild, conservation efforts are in place to ensure they survive.

"Seeing a gorilla in their natural habitat – the thick and lush rainforest on the side of a dormant volcano – was my goal. Turns out seeing the gorilla was not a challenge; getting to them proved to be, though. After a two-hour hike and hearing rustling in the bushes, we finally saw a gorilla. He was perched on a tree overlooking the valley below.

"It was an amazing sight. Then the next thing we knew, we were in amongst the Amahoro (Kinyarwandan for Peace) gorilla family. They didn't seem phased by us at all. We had an hour to take it all in. During that time, I had a close encounter with the dominant male of the group named Ubumwe. A *really* close encounter.

"Ubumwe is a little over 5 feet tall and weighs about 450 pounds. When he moved towards me, I did what I was told by the guide. I got down as low as I could and averted my eyes so as not to pose any challenge to the magnificent primate."

"All I saw when he passed by within two feet of me was black hair. Nothing else; just black hair taking up my entire field of vision. Then he walked past me, and with the group, disappeared into the bush.

Photo by Colin Wiebe

"The guide said had I not done what I was told, there was a good chance the silverback would have reached out with its massive, muscled arm and whacked me, and I would have been at the bottom of the hill before I knew what happened.

"As it was, the hour passed by in a flash, and we were on our way down the hill with stories, photographs, and memories.

Photo by Rob Hislop

"Shortly after getting home, my ability to talk led to another amazing situation. I met the now-director of the Nina Haggerty Centre for the Arts and was invited to come and speak about my visit with the gorillas to the artists' collective - a group of talented people with developmental disabilities.

"A couple of months later, we had a gallery showing called Out of the Darkness. It included my gorilla prints and works of art from the collective based on my experience.

Photo by Colin Wiebe

Photo by Rob Hislop

"I was both humbled and amazed by the people (and gorillas) I met in Rwanda, Ethiopia, at the Nina Haggerty, and those who supported the exhibit. It is still hard to believe what came out of a coffee with a good friend."

Photo by Rob Hislop

Pandemic poetry...
Chapter 26

Covid-19 cost me many bookings I had been looking forward to. I was booked for a Wellness Conference in Millet. I had spoken at such events before around the province and had some great stories to tell and poetry to share.

In December 2020, I had Christmas parties booked, and the following month I had a gig booked at the River Cree Casino.

For February of 2021, the Alberta Teachers Association had invited me to speak again (I had the year before) at their annual convention.

All would have to be cancelled.

And then there was the one for August of 2020 in Westlock, where I had already spoken at various events, including one where some had to be turned away because the hall was full.

This one, with a Ukrainian Dinner, would take some extra planning.

I was preparing to order a new puppet, Baba, to tell the story of what happened to me at a Farmer's Market when a Baba (Ukrainian for grandmother) selling pickles put me in my place. It would be an excellent example of self-deprecating humour.

This is the same story I told at the Apollo, as mentioned earlier.

I would have to get Marg to make Baba a babushka (head scarf).

I needed some Ukrainian words to make the story more fitting for the event, and I had planned to call fellow auctioneer Nick Gulka, whom I also knew as a host on CISN Country 103.9 and 840 CFCW, to teach Baba how to properly say some of the Ukrainian words he likes to throw in during his radio show.

When the show had to be cancelled, she was so disappointed the words she was thinking are probably not printable.

In any language.

Trolls

We were again under attack from those on Twitter saying our news may be slanted because we receive financial help from our federal government.

Upper management sent a Tweet: "Just going to say this again: Canadian broadcast news organizations like @globalnews @CTVNews @CityNews are not eligible for and will not receive a single cent from the Liberals' $595M journalism fund."

Came the response: "Oh, don't worry we thought about it. These companies also own printed media... so in the end yes they receive our liberal media supporter funds."

The reply from management: "None of the companies mentioned own print media outlets that would qualify either. Now run along, troll."

I wrote what I hoped would become a song about all of this:

Run along, little troll...

(Chorus)

Run along little troll, go back into your hole.

We don't need your darkest thoughts on Twitter.

Your rank conspiracies, are just adolescent cheese,

And make you Social Media litter.

Like a soiled fine-toothed comb over Twitter, you do roam,

For ways to turn good people into quitters.

The not-smarts jump aboard, hanging on your every word.

Then, they, too, pretend to be bitter.

Looking for a tweet to twist, you must keyboard with a fist,

Even if it's just a hair-splitter.

With no courage in the game, you attack under a fake name,

Making you a social media counterfeiter.

Do you think you are a smarty or work for a political party?

Do you get a decent cheque when you remit 'er?

Are you coached on what to moan, or do you do it all alone?

Do you think your pointless point makes Twitter glitter?

Will you hurt someone today with the things you've got to say?

Or will it be a sad no-hitter?

Is there no adult around to hear your keyboard pound?

I think you need a Twitter babysitter.

Mother's Day 2020

Dear Marg,

Mother's Day was coming, and the search was in vain,

For a card without the same old verses again.

I wanted a card that said what I felt,

But the Hallmark writers don't know how that's spelt.

You have been such a wonderful mother,

To our six kids, sisters and brothers,

From cook to advisor, nurse to sympathizer,

You carried the load like no one else can,

Plus made beautiful quilts and put up with your man.

It's your special day and I know what your heart wants,

To travel and see some of your favorite haunts.

But the travel police are watching our door,

To make sure we don't enjoy a trip once more.

Not even a hug from a grandchild allowed,

Stay six feet apart and don't go near a crowd.

So where can I take you to show that I care?

The government says, "Nowhere, just stay right there!"

If home's where the heart is then we'd better listen

Though a trip to *somewhere* is what we are missin'.

We can only go Nowhere, no spectacular view.

But I'll be happy in Nowhere, if I'm with you.

I love you,

Bob

As advertised...

For Easter, since we were not able to have the family over for dinner or to visit any of their homes, Marg and I decided to deliver part of their Easter meal to their doorstep.

It was a casserole of veggies and hamburger topped with Tasti Taters®.

April 10, 2020

Hi family,

We hope you are safe and well. We thought it would be nice to have an Easter brunch with you. So, while we won't be seeing you across the table, you'll be having the same as the rest of the family from Spruce Grove to Edmonton to Beaumont.

Under the golden layer of Tasti Taters, skillfully cut and shaped by Chef McCain in New Brunswick, and adorned with several cheeses, is a nutritious mixture of cut green beans with a wonderful texture from Mississauga, baby carrots carefully carried in from California, and just a hint of the best Canadian onions available in April.

These delicious vegetables are lovingly embraced in a sauce made of lean chicken and fresh sour cream, with no artificial flavours or colours.

This dish sits on a bed of lean ground beef with a dash of dill, Worcestershire sauce, and pepper.

Happy Easter! Let's hope we can do it for real next time.

With lots of love,

Mom and Dad

Editorial time...

Just days after my retirement I had several people on Twitter saying how much they wished they could hear an editorial. My brain was still writing editorials as I heard every newscast.

The thoughts were always coming fast and furious, and I'd even think of them when I'd wake up early in the morning, even though I was supposed to be retired! Old habits die hard, I guess, and I guess I'm old.

There was so much I wanted to say, so, here is what I posted on Twitter:

Limerick Editorial January 4, 2021

Would our government ever forsake us?

Stay at home without family – they make us.

The vaccine may be late,

But they don't hesitate,

To choose Hawaii or Phoenix or Vegas.

They're supposed to speak safeties to follow.

Instead, they say Luau and Mahalo.

They go on their travels,

While the economy unravels

Do what we say, not we do, sounds hollow.

A key word in politics is trust.

Without it a party goes bust.

We have to believe 'em,

There is no deceivin',

Or the blue truck drives off into the dust.

I'm really not angry, I'm jealous.

They did opposite to what they did tell us.

Rules made families cry,

As they soared into the sky.

Will you buy what they next try to sell us?

Even the Pope is condemning

Those who flee their own country like lemmings.

No thought for their actions,

As Covid infractions,

Or from where the next outbreak is stemming.

Some Albertans are ticked, mee-oh-man-o!

From Lethbridge up to Capilano

They don't want to hear "stay",

As Maui's plane flies away,

They want to hear Kenney say, "Book 'em, Dan-o!"

Let me know what you think.

I'm Bob Layton

POTUS and the pooch

March 10, 2021

Was Joe Biden's dog in the hooch?

From the White House he's ordered to scooch.

A guard he did bite,

Put on a midnight flight.

James Corden says he was impooched!

March 15, 2021

Our dates are set for vaccines.

Some tell me it's just hoax dreams.

But with 5G micro-chips

From my head to flop-flips

Cell phones should work better, it seems.

March 19, 2021

My vaccine means no more Covid cough,

My hat to the province I doff.

No side-effects trauma,

No conspiracy drama,

Oh wait – my ear just fell off!

(Last line came from brother Ralph).

March 25, 2021

Carbon tax on our gas and our crude

Government taxes are getting so lewd.

Not all judges agreed,

But filled Liberal needs

Will we also need Trudeau tattoos?

March 28, 2021

So, I woke up today and I'm 77,

Thought by now I'd be gone to heaven

Or down below

Where C-tax deniers go

Instead, I'm masking for 7-11!

April 8, 2021

We're told to cough into our elbow, I believe

And cover your face so Covid can't conceive.

Not too much to ask

Marg made me a mask

From the elbow of an old shirt sleeve!

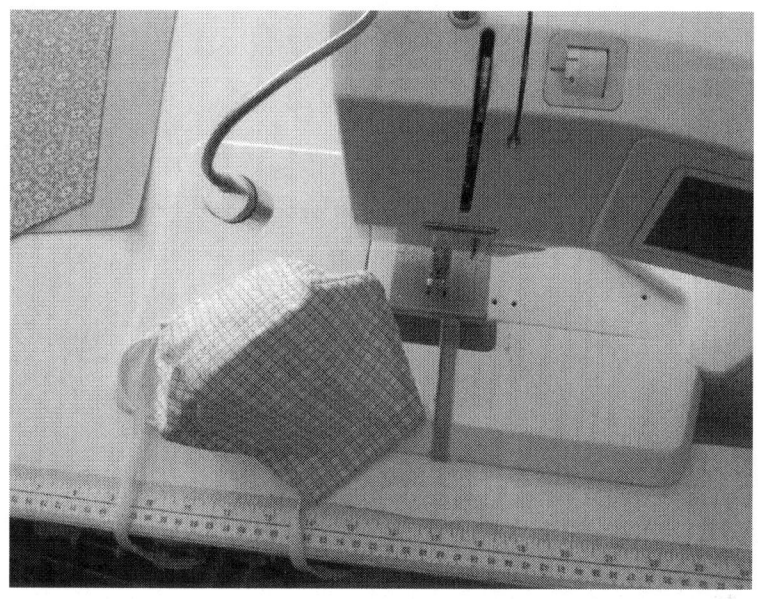

After I tweeted this out, @Lorne_Corbett replied:

A mask from a sleeve

You have to believe

Is better than briefs

Which still brings relief

Butt may be hard to perceive.

What a great morning laugh, Lorne!

The biggest response I've ever had to a tweet came when Grace Life Church was shut down and had a fence built around it. I tweeted:

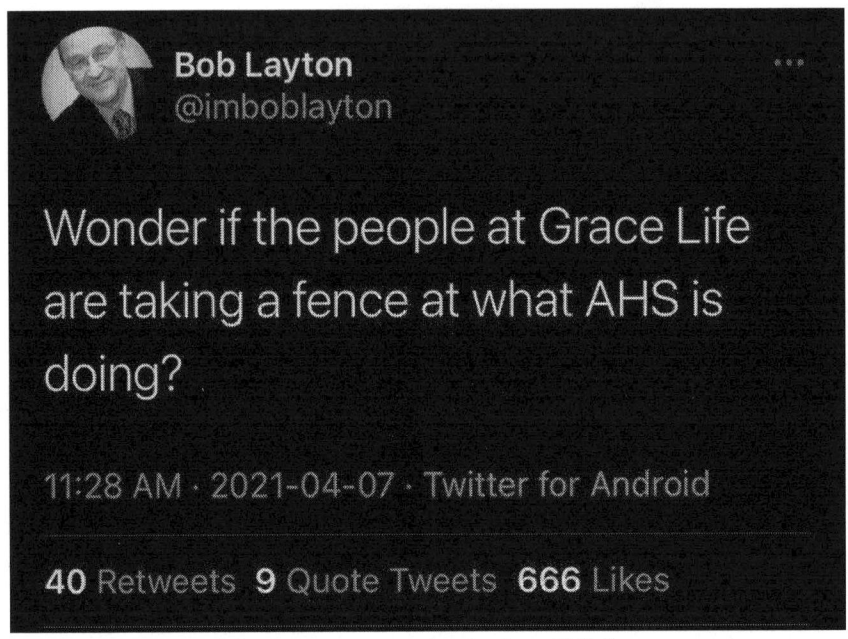

Screen capture by Arden Shibley

Arden Shibley also pointed out that at the time he took this, the Tweet had an interesting number of likes for an issue surrounding a church.

The overall response was incredible for me, at least. I received 50 Retweets, 9 Quote Tweets and 839 Likes. The Tweet activity numbers at the time of this writing were 62,011 Impressions, 71 Media views, and 5,474 Total engagements.

As Chris Sturwold tweeted: That's quite the fence... post.

Pandemic tears of joy and sadness...

Today is April 9, 2021. As I write this in the evening, it has been a morning of disappointment mixed with joy and gratefulness, and an afternoon of sadness and memories and even more disappointment, still with gratefulness around the edges. A real salad of mixed emotions.

One of the things the pandemic spoiled for Marg and I and the rest of the family and most of you reading, was the ability to travel and be with each other on special occasions.

At one point, unable to withstand the pain of not being together, we drove to southern Alberta and back for a meeting of about an hour with family. It would mean more than twelve hours of driving in one day – since we did not want to chance a motel – but it was worth it to see everyone in person instead of on a screen.

Our beautiful granddaughter, Tessa Watson, is attending university in Idaho to become a social worker. She fell in love with another student, Connor Holmes.

Today was their wedding day. Were it not for the border restrictions, we would have driven down for the wedding and had a wonderful time with them.

Instead of the wedding they wanted, they were married outside, on a small wooden platform, with no decorations and just a few people who graciously took lots of pictures and video on their cell phones.

Tessa and Connor Holmes

Yup, Watson and Holmes. I know you were thinking it.

We were not there to give them a hug, and that hurt more than we could ever realize. With the restrictions in place, we have no idea when we will ever see them in person. Still, we are grateful for their decision to press on with their lives, and for the technology that allowed us to watch.

The afternoon would be a different story. Only during a pandemic could you experience a virtual wedding you were not allowed to attend in the morning, and the virtual funeral of a friend you were not allowed to attend in the afternoon.

Her name was Monica McLaughlin.

Monica McLaughlin 1953-2021

She had arrived in Canada from Jamaica in the mid-1980s with her young, adopted son, Dwayne. Single women are permitted to adopt in Jamaica.

Monica had immigrated to be with her mother, Iris, who came to Canada in 1970.

Speaking at the celebration of Monica's life, family friend Chad Bowie said, in part:

"Monica was one of the most kind and compassionate human beings I have encountered. Monica went out of her comfort zone to let people know that they were important and loved.

"The words of Maya Angelou are applicable when reflecting on Monica. She states, 'I have learned that people will forget what you said, people will forget what you did, but people will never forget how you made them feel.'

"I will always remember how Monica made me feel. Most assuredly I am not the only one who remembers Monica for her unwavering kindness, generosity and compassion."

AWARDS

Chapter 27

Awards are wonderful to receive, but you do not win them by yourself. It is always a team effort. You need a management team that will support you when the trolls come out to try to say you meant something different than what you really said or call you a "Nazi," maybe because they can't think of anything worse.

At one point, I had to deal with complaints to the Canadian Broadcast Standards Council. I had been accused of having a "double meaning." After months of worry on my part, they determined the complaints to be "without merit."

There was also the time I received a death threat against me and my entire family. The writer threatened to kill all of us. I forwarded the email to police, and they were able to track down the person responsible. It was a teenaged boy who had done it on a dare from his friends.

Police told me they had not laid any charges, yet. They had gone to his home with a search warrant, and his parents were horrified at what he had done to satisfy his supposed "friends," when the family had a trip to Disneyland planned.

Police told me they had explained to this boy that if I wish to have them lay charges, with a criminal record he would not be allowed to cross into the United States, and his life would be changed in so many ways. They told me he seemed genuinely remorseful and scared and did not believe he posed a threat, but it was up to me if they laid charges.

I suggested they tell him I was thinking about what to do, and would let them know in about a week. During that time, I received a heartfelt letter of apology from the boy.

I responded to let him know how much fear he had caused. I explained I would not be taking this any further and suggested he be cautious in accepting any further dares.

But back to winning awards. You also need a technical team with the passion to make what you have written come to life, adding video clips and special effects, sometimes changing with every sentence.

I would record my editorials at Global TV on a Thursday, and let the editors have at it. The next day, I would see the finished product for the very first time, the same as the audience, and would often find myself talking to the TV, expressing my appreciation for what they had done. I would later email those thoughts to those responsible.

When asked once how I was able to win TV awards, I replied, "Jesus is my co-pilot."

Yes, I am a man of faith, and I would wait until their eyebrows stopped lifting and then add, "My producer is Kevin Jesus."

As for any thoughts that winning awards is a part of the glamour people in the public eye enjoy, I just saw an interview with country singer Merle Haggard. He said that while you may think being a so-called "star" is a life other people can only dream of, it can be more like just 35 years of sitting in a bus.

The equivalent for some, who just play his music, may be 35 years of getting to work at three o'clock in the morning.   Still, for me, it was a wonderful career.

Although some people would get wide-eyed and shake their head after hearing the hours I worked, it never really bothered me, it was just part of the job.

It wasn't until I hit about my 75th birthday that I felt like I was starting to slow down a little and knew the end must be near.

Let me share with you just a few of the awards and how they came to be.

The first radio award I received after 630 CHED Manager Doug Rutherford told me I was to start doing editorials (since it seemed I always had something to say, and Eddie Keen was retired) was in remembrance of the time they decided to teach sex education in schools.

This incident happened several years before I won the award and involved a note from the educators to those adults who were not sure if they wanted their child to take the class. Those parents were invited to a hall to hear a sample class and offer any feedback.

I arrived with some other parents and we took our seats.

As we waited for the session to begin, we were given a copy of the curriculum to peruse. There were sections on how to prevent the transmission of disease, how birth control worked, and so on. Try as I might, I could not find the word "abstain" as a preventive measure.

When the teacher began the meeting, she asked if there were any questions about the written material. I asked why there was not something prominently featured about abstaining from sex before marriage. What happened next shocked me.

Before the teacher could respond, the other parents assailed me. "Idiot!" "There's no point in telling kids not to do it—they're all doing it!" "Yours are probably doing it right now!" "You think they'll abstain?" "Get your head out of the sand!"

Caught by surprise, and just a little disgusted at the way I was being treated, I was at a loss for words. Not often *that* ever happened.

The teacher suggested we move into an actual lesson, and asked us to go to the other side of the room where coffee and donuts were laid out. She asked everyone to fill out a name tag and put it on and shake hands with a few people to get to know them. The rest of the group complied.

I did not.

As the teacher coaxed me to join in, a thought was strongly impressed on my mind. It was as though a mysterious voice was warning, "Don't go."

I didn't.

When the rest returned, she asked them to remove their name tags. She asked who had the one with the tiny flower she had drawn on it—the flower that represented disease. "And, which of the others did you shake hands with?" she asked.

The fellow pointed them out.

"For the purposes of the class," the teacher explained, "the handshake represents intimacy, and did you wear a rubber glove?" The symbolism was obvious. He had not, and she asked those who had shaken his hand to identify those whom they had shaken hands with. Soon it became apparent that apparently everyone in the room had been symbolically infected, and she confidently made that pronouncement.

She looked very pleased with her lesson.

The others were nodding and smiling in approval. Someone said, "Yeah, that's a good way to explain it to the kids. I like it. I like it a lot."

It was then that this mysterious voice urged me to speak up. I congratulated the teacher on a lesson well-presented but pointed out that not all of us were infected.

"How could that be?" she asked, a look of unbelief on her face.

"One of us... abstained."

The room went quiet.

Photo by Rob Hislop

Wash your hands...

Just for fun, I did a TV editorial for children, my squawky bird telling them to wash their hands for as long as it takes to sing Happy Birthday. Strangely enough, it was a health warning the media had been asked to mention. Who could have known what "wash your hands" could mean just over a decade later?

Photo by Rob Hislop

After seeing my puppet, many requests came in to entertain at children's birthday and Christmas parties. That was not for me. My show is designed for adults. There were courses in the US on how to do a children's ventriloquist show, but they were never at a time when I was available to attend.

Besides, my friends from St. Albert, known professionally as "Peter and Mary" do the best children's show I have ever seen. Mary is a ventriloquist, with a puppet that looks like her. I have no intention of competing.

Harvest Moon

With environmental issues always at the fore, we had various American celebrities visit the Fort McMurray and area Oil Sands, or the "Tar Sands," as they like to call them.

One of these people was a favorite singer of mine, ever since "Teach your children well…", Neil Young. When he finished his critique of the way Alberta does things, I offered my own critique of the way he does things. In my editorial, I told him how much I loved his music, especially "Harvest Moon," but I told him that if we ever met, I might like to show him my own *harvest moon*.

As I write this today on May 28, 2021, Global News is reporting that a longtime company in the Canadian oilpatch, the Canadian Association of Oilwell Drilling Contractors is changing its name to the Canadian Association of Energy Contractors. It is their plan to lessen its use of fossil fuels in the future, in favour of greener forms of energy.

I guess after all these years Bob Dylan is still right; the times, they are a-changin'.

Photo by Rob Hislop

It was in 2015 that the late Alberta Premier, Jim Prentice, in speaking of the provincial financial situation, suggested that if we wanted to know who was to blame, we should all "Look in the mirror." He said we always had the best of everything and did not have to pay the actual cost.

My phone was ringing. "Bob, come on – you have to say something about this. You are our voice!"

I did the editorial while looking into a hand mirror which I accidently smashed, and then suggested that when you break a mirror, it means you are going to get seven years of bad...

government. The response from the audience was great. The response from my peers was even greater.

It would bring a national award.

Photo by Rob Hislop

Do you remember all the scare stories around the transition to the year 2000? There were unfounded fears that computers around the world would fail in trying to add the new date.

Management told me I should stay on the air and do the newscast live at midnight, so we could tell people if banks or governments or airlines or whatever were in trouble. I objected, I did not believe there would be any trouble, but I was outvoted.

Also ticking me off, was that I had a New Year's Eve show booked and would have to cancel. Not happy.

In the hours leading up to midnight, as other countries struck twelve and set off the fireworks, it was obvious there were no computer problems.

I knew management was correct in having me there in case the world did start falling apart, but I took small comfort in that, since I did not believe it was going to happen.

I began to write the midnight newscast. I had to stay professional. Fact based. No obvious sarcasm.

An anchor must stay calm in the face of an emergency, and in letting the audience know there was nothing more to worry about.

Still, my midnight newscast was probably not done in the best frame of mind. However...

Photo by Rob Hislop

Bottom line: After Gary Mack or "Byron MacGregor" left this life and an award was created in his name, it was quite an honour for me to receive it.

And then, someone had to remind the new city council we lived in a "winter" city.

Photo by Rob Hislop

How many times did we report looting and burning in US cities?

What would seem to begin as a peaceful protest would escalate into what became an all-out attack on businesses.

It was interesting to hear that police in the affected cities were checking license plates to find out if the looters were from that city or even from that state, or if they were just taking advantage of the situation to break windows and haul merchandise out of the stores.

Photo by Rob Hislop

Question: Should there have been a public referendum on whether to build what is now known as Rogers Place in downtown Edmonton?

We got some angry phone calls from listeners opposed to the idea as council debated the issue.

There were arguments on both sides, but now as we see what has happened to the Ice District, there are few complaints about what this has done for downtown Edmonton.

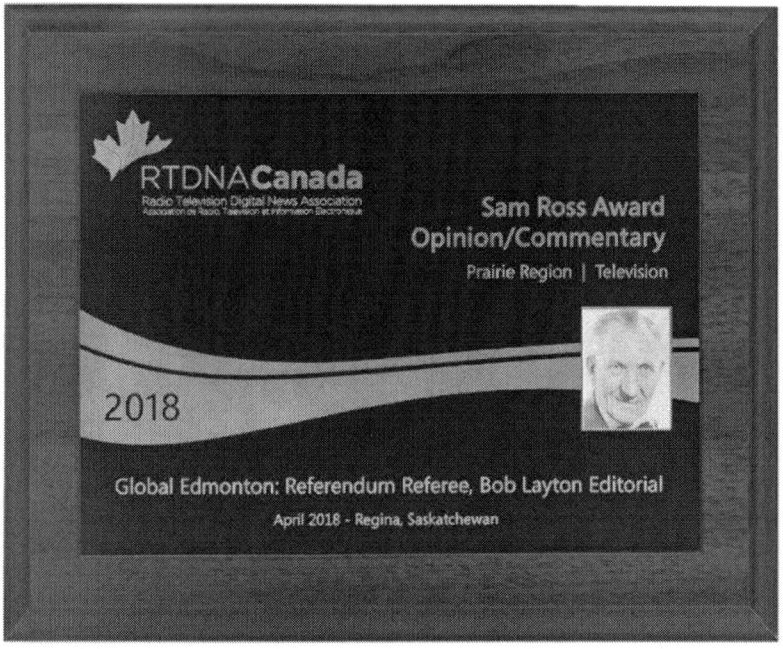

Photo by Rob Hislop

Remember all the condo fires in Edmonton, caused in several cases by the improper disposal of smoking materials? I thought there should be a law against that.

I remember well the response from listeners who disagreed with reports saying the person responsible had "accidentally" disposed of a cigarette butt in balcony potted plants. They wanted to make the point that you don't "accidentally" put it in there – you "deliberately" put it in there!

As I write this in 2021, the fires caused by the improper disposal of smoking materials continue.

Photo by Rob Hislop

There are awards that seem to have a message, at least, that's what I was left thinking. Does a Lifetime Achievement Award mean the end is near? It certainly made me think about my career in broadcasting and whether it was time to get serious about the next phase of my life.

Photo by Rob Hislop

Photo by Rob Hislop

As I said at the beginning of this chapter, you don't win awards by yourself, it's a team effort with the advice and direction of good leaders.

So, who do I owe my career to? There was my dad, who first taught me public speaking. There was my grade eight teacher,

Mr. O'Shiro, who first told me I had a flair for writing. Then it was Principal Ward Steckle, who suspended me in grade 12 from Western Canada High School in Calgary for having too much to say.

Next, it was the correspondence instructors at the Columbia School of Broadcasting in San Francisco. Then, Mel Stevenson who took a chance and gave me my first job in radio at CKNL, Fort St. John, B.C., in 1970. In 1971, Jerry Forbes and his team gave me the opportunity to work at 630 CHED. As I mentioned earlier, in 1994, 630 CHED General Manager Doug Rutherford told me to start writing editorials.

As I started doing editorials for Global TV, it was News Director Michael Fulmes who changed me from doing five "talking heads" a week to just one editorial on Fridays, but properly produced. We went from quantity to quality as the awards came in.

In the later years, as the times and the audience changed, it was Global's General Manager Jim Haskins on the TV side and Talk and Talent Director Syd Smith on the radio side who offered excellent guidance.

I was so fortunate to have this type of broadcasting mentorship.

And I owe so much to my wife, Marg, who always showed support. She could be my toughest critic and my strongest fan.

And one final thought...
Chapter 28

As a person who enjoys telling stories, it has been a real pleasure to share with you some of my life experiences.

Now, it is your turn to do the same. Think back on the most precious moments of your life and write them down. Include what you have learned about staying positive in tough times, the value of true friendship, the difference between good and bad debt, and finding a fulfilling career that does not detract from family.

Remember to include your mistakes, and remember, self-deprecating humour is usually the funniest.

Some of the best quotes will come from your children, and things they innocently say will sound great at their wedding and sometimes even at a funeral.

I remember the Thanksgiving when our children were small. We told them we wanted to start a family tradition. Since Thanksgiving was just a few days away, we would buy a turkey. They could join us in the kitchen and learn how to stuff it if they wanted and help us make some salad, and maybe a pumpkin pie.

Their response? "Eeeeww. We don't want to do that."

"Why not?" I asked. "Don't you want some turkey?"

No, they didn't, really.

"It's Thanksgiving – we should have a turkey," Marg and I coaxed.

Nope. Not interested.

"What would you rather have?" I asked, maybe a little impatiently.

"You wouldn't let us have it anyway," came the reply.

I took a deep breath. I had wanted this to be a happier day. Marg agreed. We looked at each other for a moment, and then I said, "Okay, tell me what you want for Thanksgiving dinner, and you can have it."

"Promise?"

"We promise."

Marg added, "Your dad and I will maybe just get a small turkey for us, and you can have whatever you want."

They told us what they wanted, and left Marg and I looking helplessly at each other as we agreed to their wish for a Thanksgiving dish.

With the holiday over, the children went back to school, and the next day we got a call from the school guidance counselor.

I took the call, and she asked if everything was okay at our house. I told her it was.

She asked if I was employed. I told her I worked at 630 CHED. She had never heard of me. Well, I hadn't been there that long.

She asked if we had sufficient food in the house.

I asked her what this was all about, and she explained to me that when children come back after a holiday, some teachers have them write a paragraph explaining how they celebrated it and what the family did.

Sometimes, she explained, the information they gather is so concerning they call in a social worker or even the police.

In this case, she was just making the initial call.

"So, you still haven't told me what the problem is," I said.

She told me that one of our children had printed out the words, "For Thanksgiving, our mom and dad gave us the best dinner they ever could. We had hot dogs!"

I've heard it said that humour is often just tragedy plus time. Something to keep in mind as you write down your most important memories.

If you would like some help in writing your life story, especially what you should include, and maybe what you should not, I offer a PowerPoint seminar loaded with personal stories designed to trigger your memories. I would love to visit your organization. Contact me at blayton@shaw.ca.

The things you write may be precious to the generations that follow. Remember the words of Randy Travis. In his song, "Three Wooden Crosses," he sang, "It's not what you take when you leave this world behind you, it's what you leave behind you when you go."

Whatever you've got to share, whether it leads to great riches or noticing the riches of life, I just know you've had great experiences future generations can benefit from.

I encourage you to write your own version of *I'll Puke in Your Pocket*. At the back of the book I have left a couple of pages in case you want to jot something down that has just popped into mind having heard the suggestion.

I'm... Bob Layton

Copyright

"I'll puke in your pocket!" The Side Hustles of Bob Layton

Copyright 2021 by Bob Layton. All rights reserved. No part of this publication may be used or reproduced, stored in a retrieval system, or transmitted, in any form or by any means, electronic, mechanical, photocopying, recording or otherwise, without the prior written permission of both the copyright owner and the publisher of this book.

Printed in Canada

NOTES

NOTES

Manufactured by Amazon.ca
Bolton, ON

36376820R00173